IN REAL life

westlife

THE OFFICIAL BOOK

Lise Hand

Virgin

Dedication

For Shane, Nicky, Mark, Kian and Bryan – today the world, tomorrow the Croker . . .

And

For Louis – thanks for the nest of tables . . .

This edition first published in Great Britain in 2001 by
Virgin Publishing Ltd
Thames Wharf Studios
Rainville Road
London
W6 9HA

First published in 2000 by Virgin Publishing Ltd

ISBN 0 7535 0588 6

Typeset by Phoenix Photosetting, Chatham, Kent
Printed and bound in Great Britain by
Mackays of Chatham, Chatham, Kent

Contents

Author's Acknowledgements

A huge *go raibh maith agat* to Kian, Mark, Bryan, Shane and Nicky for their kindness and chat. And to my hero, Anto Byrne, for his Job-like patience, and to Louis Walsh for his cheerful optimism that I'd get the damn thing written by the deadline.

I'd also like to thank the Westlife mums — Patricia Egan, Mae Filan, Marie Feehily, Yvonne Byrne and Mairead MacFadden for all their help.

And grateful thanks to Simon Cowell, Sharon Tobutt and Tam Oliver in RCA, and Kathryn Mason at BMG Ireland. Also to Stuart Slater and James Bennett at Virgin Publishing. And thanks to Pete Waterman, Steve Mac and Andrew Berkowitz at Arista, and everyone else who helped me.

Most of all, a serious thanks to Marge and Jim for their support, the mugs of tea and the loan of a posh computer . . .

— *Lise Hand*

List of Illustrations

Text pages:

Colour section:

Prologue
Hangin' on the Telephone . . .

Sunday 2 May 1999

It was a bright, warm afternoon, the second day of summer, but cats and dogs could have been falling out of the sky as far as the five boys from Westlife were concerned. The band were locked away in the famous PWL studio in South London, recording two songs, 'Seasons in the Sun' and 'I Have a Dream', which were to be released in time for the Christmas charts. But all that was far in the future. This particular afternoon, all Shane, Nicky, Bryan, Mark and Kian could think about was what was going to happen when the UK Top 20 charts were announced at 1 p.m.

There was a chance that their debut British single, 'Swear It Again', would go to Number One. The signs were good: the band had just performed for the first time ever on *Top of the Pops* – a show that all five of them had watched over the years while doing their homework in front of the telly in their homes in Sligo and Dublin.

Even better, 'Swear It Again' was already Number One in Ireland – it had been since the beginning of April – and was the fastest-selling debut single in Irish chart history. Since its release, Westlife had hardly slept, dashing around Britain and Ireland, doing interviews, television shows, appearances – anything to help the single to get to the top of the charts.

But now it was coming up to 1 p.m., and there was nothing more that they could do, except wait and pray. As the magic hour drew closer, the band couldn't concentrate any longer and they all piled into the studio's sitting room to wait for *the* phone call. They were sitting in leather car seats that the producer had taken from an antique Citroën car, and all five took out their mobile phones and put them on the table.

Two other men waited with them. One was the owner of the studio, the legendary producer Pete Waterman, who had made stars in the 1980s out of pop acts such as Kylie Minogue, Jason Donovan and Rick Astley, and was now scoring number one hits with bands such as Steps. The other man was their tour manager, Anto Byrne.

There was silence in the room, usually unheard of when these five boys were together. Even Shane and Bryan, who sing all day, sat quietly. They stared at the walls, which were lined with platinum and gold discs. More than anything, Westlife wanted to have their own shiny disc up there too. Nervous fingers drummed on the table, and tense feet tapped the floor. What was taking so long?

Then one of the phones suddenly chirped loudly. It was Bryan's (for once, he hadn't lost it). Everyone jumped, and Bryan dived on his phone. 'Hello? Hello?' he gasped breathlessly as the rest of the band clutched each other and waited.

Bryan's face dropped. 'Mum, Mum – you've gotta get off the phone – *now*! We're waiting for the call. Yes, yes, I'll ring. I promise,' he said urgently. He looked at the others: 'Sorry about that, lads,' he said sheepishly.

Almost at once, another phone rang. It was Kian's. He snatched it up: 'Hello?' Then he heard the voice of the band's manager, Louis Walsh, shouting down the line, 'You're Number One! I knew you'd do it! You're Number One!'

Pete immediately ran upstairs to pop the cork on a big bottle of champagne. Even now, the band weren't sure how to react. They jumped up and all hugged each other, but were lost for words. It was almost too much to take in – it had taken their heroes Boyzone five attempts to top the UK charts before they succeeded with 'Words'.

But now 'Swear It Again' was Westlife's first Number One. Little did they think on that Sunday afternoon that in the coming months a string of chart topping singles would propel them into the record books. Nor could Shane Filan have dreamed that he would celebrate his 21st birthday the following year by singing 'Swear It Again' with the owner of Harrods, Mohammed al-Fayed, when they were invited to open the world-famous store's sale.

None of them knew that they had just climbed on the maddest merry-go-round in the world.

Kian says, 'None of us imagined that we had a chance of getting to Number One in the UK so fast. We were all amazed when "Swear it Again" topped the Irish charts, and thought that was as good as it gets. When Louis told me that he was going to try to get our first single to the top in Britain, I just laughed at him.

I thought he was mad, and told him that, if by some miracle we made it into the top twenty, we'd all be thrilled. And when the midweek charts came out in Britain that week, and showed us to be in the number-one spot, we were ecstatic but really nervous. It kept going round and round in our heads all the time, because we wanted it more than anything. And that Sunday in the studio, the waiting was unbearable. We were just dying for the phone to ring – and then Bryan's mum nearly gave us a heart attack. Just after one o'clock, Louis rang and next thing we were all jumping around like lunatics! But anyone who thinks that we all went out on a mad celebration that night is sadly mistaken. We all had an early night, because we were on a plane at dawn the next morning!'

Mae Filan (Shane's mum) says, 'It was really tense that week, waiting for the Sunday charts. The phone was constantly ringing, with people asking, "Any news yet?" But the boys were great. As soon as they heard from Louis, they all rushed out and phoned home. Then all the families phoned each other, and then all of us met up with Mark and Kian's families and friends, as we all live quite close to each other in Sligo and we went to a local hotel to celebrate. We were all having a great time and phoned the boys from the hotel to say hello – and they were all in bed asleep!'

Mairead MacFadden (Bryan's mum) says, 'Poor Bryan couldn't get me off the phone quick enough! But I just wanted to know.'

Westlife: In Real Life

Kian's School Essay: 'What It Would Be Like To Be Famous'

Today I sat in class by the window looking at the fields, thinking about absolutely nothing. The night before I just had a practice with the band. I hope we're gonna make it.

When you think of it, its not that hard, all you have to do these days, is get a good song and we have loads of good songs.

Suddenly I just started thinking of the girls screaming, asking you for autographs, and boldly throwing themselves at you. Imagine sitting in the limo on your way to play in the biggest concert hall in the world. When you get there, the door opens, and all you can hear is girls screaming at the top of their voices and all you can see are flashes of cameras and video and TV cameras. As we walk through the barriers, the fans were totally losing their heads.

It was half an hour before the time we hit the stage. We are sitting in the dressing room, getting our voices in order and going over the dance steps. We are totally excited and can't keep control of ourselves.

When our manager came in, she said that this would be the biggest and best concert of our lives. This is what we had worked for and we weren't gonna mess it up now.

By this stage, sitting in the classroom back at real life, I was totally and utterly in a trance thinking of this concert and there was no way I was gonna stop there. It was too good a dream.

We were on our way to the stage and we were pure excited. When we walked on the light in the whole place went down, and we got into position for the first song. We were deafened by the screams and my heart was about to jump out of my body. After the first few songs we had settled down. Now it was the big test. It was my turn to sing solo and my nerves were killing me. After the song I never heard more screams in all my life.

After the concert we went back to the dressing room and we were never happier. It was time to go and meet the lucky fans that got to go backstage. We signed autographs for about half an hour. We were in full swing now and weren't stopping. Next thing I know, I get a tap on the shoulder. It was one of my classmates telling me that class was over.

As I walked on my way to the next class, I just couldn't stop thinking about just what it would be like to be famous.

– KIAN, AGED 13

Teacher's comment: 'You kept to the title, Kian. But only covered one side. What about negative sides like drugs, drink etc . . .

1 The Early Years – Football and Flying Monkeys

As far as rock and pop music is concerned, Dublin is the Capital of Cool: U2 are all Dubs, as are Samantha Mumba, the gals from B*Witched and the guys from Boyzone. (OK, so the Corrs are from the town of Dundalk, which is an hour's drive from Dublin. But nobody's perfect.)

And until two years ago pop stars most certainly did not come from Sligo. It is a modest town on the northwest coast of Ireland, surrounded by mountains and lakes, which is famous mainly for being the birthplace of the poet William Butler Yeats, who was born long before there were pop charts.

Yet in 1998, Three Wise (sort of) Men (well, boys) would follow their star from Sligo in the west to Dublin in the east, bearing gifts of great voices, cute faces and fierce determination. Shane Filan, Mark Feehily and Kian Egan have put their hometown firmly on the map. With the help of two Dubs, Nicky Byrne and Bryan MacFadden, of course . . .

Shane Filan

Shane Steven Filan made his first public appearance when he entered the world on 5 July 1979, born to Mae and Peter Filan. He was the youngest of seven – he has three older brothers and three older sisters – and grew up as the baby of the family. He describes himself as being 'incredibly close' to the rest of the clan, in particular to his sister Denise, who looks like his twin, and he loved being the youngest: 'I got away with all sorts of devilment.'

Mae and Peter have run a restaurant, the Carlton Café, for over thirty years. It's a busy and welcoming haven slap-bang in the centre of town, where shoppers drop in for a refreshing cuppa and to catch up on the local news, and where young people hang out after school. All of the Filan kids helped out in the family business during their school holidays – Shane sometimes worked behind the counter until two in the morning.

But, as a youngster, Shane was at his happiest when he was sitting on a horse, or running around a playing field – he and his brothers and sisters were mad about sports. Just about every spare inch of the Filan's sitting room is crammed with trophies, medals and plaques for showjumping, rugby, Irish dancing – Shane's sister Mairead has won several world Irish dancing championships, and Shane captained the province's Under-16 rugby team for two years.

'Growing up around horses was wonderful,' says Shane. 'There's nothing like the feeling of freedom when you're out in the fresh air, cantering cross-country. Horses are just like humans in a way, and working with them teaches you a lot about life and about building relationships. I still feel the same. My parents bought me a beautiful four-year-old gelding for my twenty-first birthday last July, and I'm dying for a chance to become friends with him.'

While Shane loves horses, he confesses that, when growing up around them, he always preferred to deal with the front end than the back end. 'I loved feeding and watering them, but I wasn't crazy about mucking out their stables. I left all that to Dad and my brother Liam. They'd do all the hard work while I went riding. I'm a bit lazy, I have to admit.'

But it wasn't all play and no work — several shelves in the family sitting room are groaning under the weight of showjumping trophies brought home by a young Shane.

'The competitions would run all winter, and it was great fun. I'd meet up with all my mates who had horses too. I competed in the pony classes, but then left it as singing took over.'

According to his mum, Shane showed signs of being a child star from an early age. In the Filan treasure box she keeps a black microphone that he made for himself when he was about four.

'He was always singing into the mike,' says Mae proudly. 'He used to sing Billy Joel songs at first, and then he moved on to Michael Jackson. Eventually, he took over the room at the very top of the house, where he could sing out loud to his heart's content without waking everyone up. He'd tell me he was going upstairs to study biology, and I'd walk in and find him writing songs!'

Shane admits that when it came to school he was a

grade-A student – in daydreaming. 'I was never mad into school. I never wanted to be a doctor or lawyer or anything like that, although when I was younger I wanted to be an astronaut – there must have been stars in my eyes from the start . . .

'I liked school but I just didn't bother studying. I spent most of my study time listening to Michael Jackson and Backstreet Boys – on my Walkman, so Mum and Dad couldn't hear me. I'd just sing along, and wonder what it would be like to be in a famous band and be able to stand on a big stage, singing a hit song. Or I'd watch videos on MTV and think, Oh God, could I ever do that? Luckily for me, I fell on my feet when I left school, as the band started to happen. I did study marketing and accounting in college in Limerick for a while, so at least I had an option if the band didn't work out. It's always good to have an option.'

Although his dad, Peter, sang in a couple of showbands and loved music (Shane grew up to the sounds of old-timers such as Jim Reeves and Joseph Locke giving it loads on the family record player), none of the children except for Shane was lured to the stage by the smell of greasepaint and the roar of the crowd.

'I was the black sheep of the family!' laughs Shane. 'I had to sing that line when we recorded "Seasons in the Sun", which I found a bit weird!'

But naturally his mum doesn't see her green-eyed youngest son as a black sheep. 'Shane was always very determined to succeed in anything he turned his attention to, whether it was rugby, kick boxing, acting or singing,' says

Mae. 'I could see that his heart was in the music business, and I never doubted that he'd make his mark. But I never thought it would all happen so quickly.'

Mark Feehily

To reach Mark's home, you have to drive out of Sligo town, turn off a main thoroughfare and follow the twists and turns of a winding country road for a few miles, until you reach a comfortable bungalow, perched amid peace and quiet on the top of a steep slope.

This is the home in which Marcus Michael Patrick Feehily – born on 28 May 1980 – grew up, the eldest son of Marie and Oliver. He has two younger brothers, Barry and Colin, respectively five and ten years his juniors. Unlike Shane and Kian, who were 'townies', Mark was surrounded by rolling green fields and was faced with one hell of a walk to get to the nearest corner shop or video store.

Not that this bothered Mark for a minute. 'I'm close to my immediate family, of course, but I'm also close to my cousins as well, as they were among the few people of my own age in the area. Both our sets of parents worked all day, so we'd all go to our granny's house after school and play together.'

In fact, Mark wasn't much bothered by the bright lights at all: 'Until I went to secondary school, which is in the centre of Sligo, I didn't go into the town much. A trip into town to do something like get a takeaway was a bit of a treat! We weren't all hillbillies coming down from the top of a mountain or anything, but we just found plenty of things to do in our own patch.'

Mark reckons he was 'a good child', but also admits that he could be 'a bit of a brat' as well. 'I'd sometimes cry when I wasn't getting my own way, and Mum was so kind-hearted that she'd just end up buying me the toy or the comic — but I wasn't completely spoiled, like one of those kids you'd just love to pick up and shake!'

But he didn't get things *all* his own way, as he vividly remembers from his first day at school: 'At the start, I went through stages of not wanting to go to school whatsoever. I think it was because there weren't that many people living in our area, so I wasn't used to being put into a roomful of strangers.

'My dad had to bring me right into the classroom, and my head would be buried in his chest and I'd be clinging to him. I'd have a woolly hat pulled down over my face, and I wouldn't even look at the teacher — all I wanted was for the teacher to go away and for me to run out into the car and go home. But I got used to it, and, half an hour into the school day, I'd be throwing pieces of paper around the room, totally fine again!'

Discovering music changed Mark's life. According to his mum, Marie, he was 'mad about singing since he was three years old. He was always the life and soul of the house, always on the go. He'd be rushing in and out, off to a tennis match, or to play badminton, and trying to fit in a bit of study in between!'

There was no great tradition of music in the Feehily household, although Mark's dad, Oliver, did have a huge record collection. 'There was loads of stuff,' remembers

Mark. 'He'd listen to bands like Queen, and mad-looking singers like Nana Mouskouri!'

Mark joined the National Children's Choir, and also learned to play the tin whistle. 'The teachers always used to send us home on Friday afternoons with a new tune to learn on the whistle over the weekend, but I'd always arrive in on Monday with some song I'd made up myself. There was always music going on in my head. If I wasn't listening to it, I was singing or writing songs. But I never for a moment thought that it was possible to do that kind of a thing for living.'

Kian Egan

Kian John Francis Egan was born on 29 April 1980. He was right in the middle of seven children, which could explain why he made more noise than the rest of his brothers and sisters together. 'I was just a bubble of energy when I was younger. It'd be eleven o'clock at night, and I'd still be running around like it was nine in the morning. I must have driven my poor mum mad!'

Quite the opposite – in fact, his mum Patricia drove Kian everywhere. 'She signed me up for all sorts of classes when I was in school. I had jazz dancing on a Monday night, tap dancing on Tuesdays, basketball on Wednesdays, piano lessons on Thursdays, guitar lessons on Fridays, speech and drama on Saturday mornings, followed by some other type of dancing in the afternoons. It was crazy, but Mum never forced me to do anything I didn't like.'

And the rest of his family were always on hand to fill up

any small gaps of free time. His brother Gavin taught him piano and guitar, his sister Fenella loved acting and got him involved in musicals, and Vivienne made sure that he looked at the odd schoolbook from time to time!

'We all got on very well,' says Kian, 'but I shared a room with Tom and we were forever beating each other up, but because he was four years older than me he was always the one who got punished!'

And if trouble loomed Kian found it useful to turn on the waterworks. 'I was very good at crying myself out of situations. When I was about ten, I smoked a cigarette trying to be cool, and ended up getting sick in our back garden! Mum caught me and started giving out yards, while I stood there crying my eyes out. So she just gave up, and told me to learn from the experience.'

Nor was Kian the only musical talent in the Egan home. 'The whole family loves music. Gavin has a master's degree in piano and guitar and teaches in Sheffield; Tom is an architect, but he also plays bass in a Sligo band, Fiction; Marielle plays violin and piano and dances and sings. Even my five-year-old brother Colm keeps asking when he's going to be given piano lessons.'

Kian is totally grateful to his parents for setting him on the road to Westlife. 'Dad's attitude has always been one of "Let's forget about buying a big house or fancy car, and let's get our kids through college and give them every advantage." And every afternoon at four o'clock, when I'd finished my homework, Mum would put me in the car and drive me to one lesson or the other. Over the years, I've played piano, guitar, clarinet, flute, bass guitar — I even played the drums for a short while, just to add to the noise!'

Nicky Byrne

Christmas has always been Nicky's favourite time of the year, when his whole extended family came together under the one roof. Born in Dublin on 9 October 1978, Nicholas Bernard James Adam Byrne was the middle of Yvonne and Nikki's three children — he has a sister, Gillian, a couple of years older than he is, and a brother, Adam, about twelve years younger.

'Christmas was brilliant in our house,' says Nicky. 'I've loads of cousins, and we all go to my grandparents with armfuls of presents, which we pile under the tree and the pile ends up halfway across the room. We have great fun opening them all in the evening. There's singing and everyone has a laugh.'

Nicky grew up very close to all his family, but there were some bits of family life that left him cold: 'My sister used to be a champion Irish dancer, and I was always being dragged to see her in competitions, which I found really boring.'

To make up for the torture of sitting through several hours of watching lads and lassies hopping about on a stage (and this was before Riverdance made Irish dancing cool — well, *coolish*), Nicky's dad took him to local football matches, or for a stroll around the Natural History Museum in the city.

'There was a huge carcass of a whale hanging from the ceiling, which used to fascinate me, along with loads of butterflies in glass cases.'

Nicky remembers his first day at school — for all the wrong reasons! 'I got knocked down on my road by a guy on a bike and was carted off to hospital. So I missed the first week of school; by the time I made it in, everyone else had settled down, and I was the only new boy! But my best mates in school are still my closest friends now — we grew up together, went to discos together, got into fights together! Even now, if I'm on tour in Asia, they'll ring me at all sorts of mad hours. It could be mid-afternoon in Dublin, and they're roaring down the phone at me to get out of bed, even though it's four a.m. where I am!'

He explains that he 'did and didn't like school', adding, 'I wasn't hugely interested in school, but I was a bit of a charmer, and got on very well with all the teachers. I was always messing in class, but I knew when to stop before I got into serious trouble. And the fact that I played football meant that some of them might have been easier on me. The teacher I always got sent to if I got into trouble was also the football team manager, and when I'd turn up to be punished for something, he'd usually say, "Never mind that — we've got a big game coming up this week!"'

At an early age, Nicky proved to be a talented footballer and quickly established himself as a promising goalkeeper. 'It was my life. Dad brought me to the mini-leagues of our local club, Home Farm, when I was six, and I went on to play for the club for eight years.'

And it gave the young Dubliner a taste of the globetrotting to come: 'We played all over Europe, and I also went on to play for Ireland in the under-fifteen, under-sixteen and under-eighteen teams. Then, when I was sixteen, I signed to Leeds.'

Nicky moved out of home on 28 June 1995. 'My mum said that she really wanted me to finish school before I left for Leeds, and looking back I think she was right. But the club was chasing me very seriously and she eventually said, "I'll give you my blessing to go, but promise me that if it doesn't work out you'll go back to school and do your Leaving Cert [A levels]." Which is exactly what I did.'

By this stage, Nicky was going out with Georgina Ahern — he had spotted her the first day he went to school in Baldoyle. However, it was a few years before he plucked up the courage to ask her out — or at least, get a pal to ask her out on his behalf. 'She said no. I was gutted!'

Eventually another friend of Nicky's approached her again, and this time she agreed to meet him. 'Our first date was at a house party, on the night before my birthday, October 8. We got on straightaway.' But then Nicky had to face another nerve-racking encounter, with Georgina's dad, Bertie Ahern, the Irish Prime Minister, who was the Minister for Finance at the time. 'I was really nervous meeting her dad for the first time. We were eating together at a local hotel, the Skylon, and I was trying to remember which cutlery to use! Then the soup came along and he dived into it with his bread roll, and I was able to relax. And, luckily, he's a huge sports fan, so we were able to talk about football.'

At first, life in Leeds was great. 'When I first signed for the club, my wages were forty-eight pounds a week, but after three months, when I signed professionally, I was earning three hundred a week – which was a fortune for a young fella – and living in great digs with other players.'

But then the going got rough. 'We were moved out of our digs into accommodation on the training ground, which was miles outside the city, and where all we did was train or hang around our rooms. Also, living away from home was getting to me. And although I was working my socks off at training, I wasn't holding down a regular place in the team.'

Nicky's career received two blows: 'I broke my elbow while I was training for Ireland for a game against Chile. I had to have an operation on it, and I had to miss three months' football. Even though I got back playing, I honestly think I never regained the form I had before my injury.'

And then the axe fell. In January 1997, two years after signing, he was called into the manager's office. 'The club had always warned me that my height was against me as a goalkeeper — I was five foot seven when I joined, and grew to five foot ten. So that day the manager told me that, unless I grew another few inches before my contract was up in June, they would have to let me go.'

Sadly, no amount of hanging off wardrobe doors could save him. The club wanted a six-foot-plus-sized goalie. 'I thought, This isn't for me. Some lower-division clubs wanted me, but I decided to go home, finish my Leaving Cert and try to get into the police force. I thought it would be a really exciting job — I still love watching police cars race by with their sirens on!'

But he admits that being let go from Leeds was 'a real kick in the stomach. Football meant everything to me, and I couldn't believe my dream was gone. But by then music was taking over.'

Could Nicky go on to become the first footballer in history to make a decent pop record?

Bryan MacFadden

Bryan's mum, Mairead, is the first to admit: 'When Bryan is singing in the house, the whole street can hear him.' Bryan was born in Dublin on 12 April 1980, and he and his sister Susan were both on stage almost as soon as they were old enough to toddle on unaided.

'I loved growing up in Dublin, and my life was very simple when I was young. I'd go to school, then the first thing I'd do when I got home was dump everything and run outside and play football with my mates. I loved football. When I was indoors, I'd listen to music, eat and sleep. That was it!'

When he was four, he joined the famous Irish singing and dancing school for kids, the Billie Barry Stage School, but was a bit too young to get fully involved. 'I left after a few weeks, but rejoined when I was eight. It was Easter time and they had a singing competition, which I entered. I came first, and won an Easter egg. When I was nine, I went for an audition for a part in *The Wizard of Oz*. I played a flying monkey, and got to whiz around above the stage, which was one of the best experiences that I've ever had. You could say that playing a flying monkey changed my life!'

And then there was school: Bryan went to St David's Primary, but, unfortunately for him, so did his mum. 'She was the secretary at the school, so I had to try to stay out of trouble, as the teachers would just threaten to send me to her, rather than to the school principal. It was usually enough to stop me messing in class!'

Thankfully for Bryan, his mum didn't follow him into secondary school, but education still wasn't much fun. 'I hated school. I used to get a bit of hassle from some people when they found out that I was going to Billie Barry, which they reckoned was really uncool. But I didn't really care. School was just a background thing, because I was so into music.'

At the same time, Bryan was no dummy. 'I did my Leaving Certificate, so I would have something to fall back on if the music didn't work out. But I left two of the exams early to go and rehearse with the band I was in at the time – I just sat there and drew pictures and wrote songs. But I still got four Bs and three Cs in honours papers – enough to qualify me to study law.'

It turned out that Bryan was something of a brain box: 'When we were in sixth year, we had to do aptitude tests that showed your intelligence and your work rate. I had the second-highest intelligence level in the school but the fourth-lowest work rate! The teachers always used to say to me, "If you pull up your socks, you could be a doctor." And I'd tell them, "I don't want to be a doctor: I want to be a singer." They'd tell me I was just a dreamer, 'cos so few people make it in show business, but I knew I could make it. Only one teacher, Miss Duggan, said, "Bryan, follow your heart. You should do what you think is right."

'I was thinking about going to study law in Letterkenny in County Donegal, which is where my dad Brendan is from. I didn't want to go to one of the big universities in Dublin, where everybody took life seriously. I wanted to have a laugh — I loved the idea of doing law, but I hated reading books, which could've been a problem!'

Profile: Kian

FULL NAME:	**Kian John Francis Egan**
DATE OF BIRTH:	**29 April 1980**
STAR SIGN:	**Taurus**
MUM AND DAD:	**Patricia and Kevin**
BROTHERS/SISTERS:	**Vivienne, Gavin, Fenella, Tom, Marielle and Colm**
HEIGHT:	**5ft 10in**
COLOUR OF EYES:	**Blue**
ANY SCARS OR TATTOOS?	**One small scar under my right eye**

What do the rest of Westlife think of Kian?

Nicky: Kian's very businesslike. He's got his head screwed on, and just loves the whole business side of the music industry. He's incredibly dedicated to the band – he'll always check that everyone is looking right. He's not afraid to air his opinion if he thinks your jeans are crap!

Mark: Kian's very serious about the band – he'd lose a leg for it, I suspect! He can be very charming, especially when there are girls about! He loves being on stage and gets a huge buzz out of it. He's very dedicated, but he also knows how to have a laugh.

Bryan: Kian is the hot-headed engine of the band: he keeps us going, even when we might be knackered. He'd do anything for Westlife, and loves the day-to-day running of the band, talking to Louis and dealing with the record companies. He's got a bit of a hot temper, though!

Shane: We've been friends for years, and we see things quite similarly. I've always been close to him and we even went out with the same girls – but not at the same time! Kian works really hard, and worries about the band a lot. He worries a lot about his hair as well! Kian has an angelic smile – which doesn't always hide the cheeky devil inside! He's happiest when he's standing on a stage in front of thousands of screaming fans, or talking business down the phone with Louis Walsh, or standing in the middle of a crowd of beautiful girls! And when Kian's not working he loves to shop – and Los Angeles is his fave hunting ground. He recently splashed out on a five-thousand-pound Rolex, and has a weakness for leather jackets, leather trousers and [he sighs] diamond rings. A girl's best friend . . .

Kian in his own words

The best moment of my life: I've tried to pinpoint one particular day, but I can't! It's always been my dream to be in a band like this. It's been my goal since I was a little kid to walk on to a stage and have thousands of people singing along to our songs.

My ideal girl: Physically, I don't have an ideal girl. But she would have to be someone I can really love and spend every moment of my life with, and not get bored. Someone I can wake up beside in the morning and say to her, 'You're the love of my life' and still be able to say it ten years later. It's easy to be head-over-heels in love with someone for a few months, but only time will tell if it's the real thing. I believe in lust at first sight, but not love. How can you love someone you don't know?

My perfect day: I'd get up early, go for a long drive in my Porsche with the roof down – it's a hot summer day. Then I'd have a game of golf with some friends, then a big family dinner. After that, I'd fly into London and Westlife would play to a packed Wembley. And then party all night with my family and friends.

My maddest part-time job: I worked as a kissogram for a while. Someone asked me to do it for a laugh, and I thought, Why not? I had to wear see-through trousers, a dicky bow and boxer shorts. It wasn't a strip or anything like that! I'd get information about the person who was getting the kissogram, and I would make up a poem about them. I'd go into the pub, drag them into the middle of the floor, read the poem, give them a kiss on the cheek – and then walk out the door with anything from sixty to a hundred pounds in my back pocket! I suppose it gave me early experience of writing lyrics, making money and coping with screaming girls!

Q&A

Who is your best friend in the band?
I don't really have one. Shane or Nicky.
Are you a morning person or a night owl?
Night owl.
Do you read your horoscope?
No.
Do you believe in aliens? If so, what do you imagine they look like?
No.

What was the first record you ever bought?
'Glory of Love', by Peter Cetera.
How useful are you in the kitchen? What can you rustle up if you have to?
I'm very good – spaghetti Bolognese is my speciality.
What part of your body would you change, if you could (keep it clean, lads)?
None – I'm happy with what I've been given.
Would you consider cosmetic surgery?
No.
Are you ticklish? If so, where (careful now)?
Yes – everywhere!
What is the most expensive thing you've ever bought?
My car.
What is the most useless thing you've ever bought?
Nothing, really.
What is the worst present you've ever received?
I've never really got a bad present.
Have you ever been in hospital?
Yes, for a broken finger.
What is your favourite breakfast?
Irish fry-up.
Hangover cures – what is the most effective?
I don't get them, believe it or not.
If you went on a blind date, who would you most like to find sitting on the bar stool?
Someone I can get along with.
Have you ever written poetry?
Yes – it's now a song.

Westlife: In Real Life

What is your favourite TV programme?
Friends.
What is your favourite item of clothing?
I've about ten favourites.
What is your most embarrassing item of clothing?
I've got some funny boxers!
What scares the living daylights out of you?
Losing my family.
What is the last thing you lost?
My mobile phone.
What is your favourite smoochy record?
I've loads of favourites.
You've recorded with Mariah – who's next for a duet (or sextet, whatever)?
Janet Jackson.
Who is your favourite musician/actor/actress?
Backstreet Boys/Brad Pitt/Cameron Diaz.
What are the best films you have ever seen?
Titanic and *Patch Adams*.
What is the best book you have ever read?
Tuesdays with Morrie by Mitch Albom.
Are you superstitious?
Not really.
Did you enjoy school? What was your favourite subject?
Kind of – I loved art.
What false name have you used in the past when checking into a hotel?
Mr Big!

Do you have a lucky charm? If so, what is it?
No.

Are you romantic?
Yes.

Have you ever had your heart broken? If so, when, and by whom?
When I was sixteen, by my first real girlfriend Sonya. We went out together for one-and-a-half years.

How old were you when you had your first kiss? Did you enjoy it?
I was nine! I didn't like it – it was too sloppy!

Where is your favourite place in the world?
Los Angeles.

Do you sing in the shower?
No.

Do you lose your temper easily?
Yes.

Do you cry easily?
Yes.

What is the worst job you ever had?
Selling tickets.

What is your favourite sport to watch and/or play?
Basketball.

If you weren't in a band, what do you think you'd be up to?
I'd be on a stage anyway, either acting or involved in music.

What do you imagine your life will be like in ten years' time?
You never can tell!

2 Musical Youths – IO YOU, Cartel and Karaoke

Growing up in the 1980s was a cool time for music lovers. If you were brave enough, you could put on frilly shirts or make-up, and warble along to Spandau Ballet or Boy George. You could mosh to metal bands such as Megadeth, get gothic with the Cure, get gloomy with the Smiths, get luvved up with the Happy Mondays or the Stone Roses, get poppy with Kylie or you could 'beat it' with Michael Jackson. You could rap with the Beastie Boys and clank around in lots of silly-looking jewellery, or play air guitar with U2 (and try to save the world at the same time).

Or you could form your own band.

In the 1980s, U2 inspired legions of Irish lads to put together four-piece rock bands and perform meaningful songs about war, peace, religion and relationships. In the 1990s, it was the turn of the boy bands and gal groups – East 17, Backstreet Boys, Take That, the Spice Girls, All Saints and, most importantly, Boyzone – to sing about broken hearts and falling in love, and to inspire a generation of wannabe popsters.

All over the world, teenagers tuned into MTV, local radio

stations and TV music shows such as *Top of the Pops*. They read pop mags such as *Smash Hits*, stuck posters of hunks and babes on their bedroom walls and snapped up CDs of their heroes. And our heroes, living happily in Sligo and Dublin, were also dancing to a different beat . . .

Shane

Shane had something of an unusual introduction into the wacky world of showbiz. 'My first time on a stage, I was dressed as a little girl! I was in a production of the musical, *Annie Get Your Gun*, and I was playing one of the little sisters, I think. I had a bonnet on me, and a little dress! Someone videoed the show, which I'd love to get my hands on!'

Dressing up in women's clothes didn't appeal to Shane, but singing and dancing definitely did. 'I didn't want to be getting girls' roles all the time – in case I got too good at it! But my first time playing a fella was in a production of *Grease*, and myself and a girl called Olwyn sang a duet, "We Go Together". It was my first time singing on a proper stage, in front of a crowd, and I just loved it!'

This was a big moment for Shane, when he first glimpsed what he might do with his life: 'That first night, I was very nervous before I went on stage, but as soon as I started singing my nerves went straight out the window. The buzz of the performance and the applause just got to me – it was just an amazing feeling, and I knew straightaway that this was what I wanted to do with my life. I realised that my best talent was singing, and I began to wonder if I could make a career out of it.'

But at first Shane couldn't decide whether he wanted to be in front of a camera or behind a microphone: 'I thought about singing, and then about acting. I always loved Tom Cruise films like *Top Gun*, and he was a bit of a role model.' And the fact that Shane looks more than a little like the fab Tom Cruise probably had something to do with it!

However, he managed to be both practical and star-struck at the same time: 'I figured out that at least ninety per cent of actors don't break into the big time, and only a hand-ful of them are well paid. I didn't fancy ending up broke and starving, so then I thought that I might try to go full time into musicals. It was about this time that Boyzone were having massive success everywhere with their second album, *A Different Beat*, and I reckoned that there wasn't room for another Irish boy band. So I was still thinking the whole thing over.'

But then the first inkling of his future career came along. 'By this time, I knew Mark, and he came up to me one day and said he wanted to go on an Irish TV talent show, called *Go For It*, and he wanted us to go on and do a song together. It never happened, but it was the first time we had thought of doing something like that. Myself and Mark and Kian had become friends through doing musicals together, and one night, around the time of *Grease*, we just sat down together and started singing Boyzone and Take That songs. It just sounded really special.'

Mark

The acting bug also nibbled at Mark when he was very young. 'When I was about ten years old, I was taken to see the musical, *Oliver!* I couldn't believe what I was seeing. I was literally getting shivers down my spine, looking up at the stage, and I so wanted to be up there with them.'

Over the next few years, the bug gnawed away at a dazzled Mark. 'I went to loads of shows after that, such as *Grease* and *The Little Shop of Horrors*, and I'd be wriggling in the seat, dying to hop up on the stage. It never occurred to me that I could have walked backstage and asked to be in the next show, as the theatres were always looking for new people!'

But then school came to the rescue, as the drama teacher simply announced that auditions were being held and all were welcome. 'I was first through the door! I found the first audition very embarrassing, as I had to sing while a teacher played the piano and everyone else stood around listening. But he didn't throw me out!'

Far from being shown the door, Mark sometimes found himself rushing from one show to the next: 'I could be in a choir or a band, a school play or a show in town, all at the same time! But I got to know everyone through the musicals – I was quite reserved and shy in school up to this point, but the shows gave me great confidence.

'I became friendly with Shane and Kian through the musicals. I knew them both before that of course, but I wasn't hanging around with them at that point – they used to be part of a cool gang, and they were very popular with the girls. But on the last night of *Grease* we were at a party, drinking away and singing songs and telling jokes. Then six of us started harmonising on the Boys II Men song, "I'll Make Love To You", and someone turned around and said, "That sounds really good. You should be in a band." So we thought we'd give it a try.'

And so the first step was taken. Mark, Shane, Kian and three other friends, Graham Keighron, Michael Garrett and Derek Lacey, formed Six As One, and did what they thought would be a one-off gig at a local hotel. But then they decided to get a bit serious: 'We changed our name to IO YOU, which we thought was catchier, and we wrote and recorded our own single, "Together Girl Forever", which sold about two thousand copies in Sligo.'

But still Mark wasn't entirely convinced that putting all his energy into performing in a band was the way to fame and fortune: 'I was looking at other options. If the band had come to an end, I was thinking about training as a teacher – I'd love the challenge of dealing with the class brats! – or maybe do social work, or something with computers. Even when IO YOU had packed out the local theatre, the Hawk's Well, for four or five nights, I was still sure the whole thing was going to come to an end.'

Kian

There were no such doubts in the busy brain of Kian Egan, who was a winner from the first moment that he stepped on to a stage: 'I was four when I took part in a local competition. The trouble was, I had an ear infection and my temperature was over a hundred! I went straight from the doctor's surgery on to the stage, recited my little poem and collected the winner's cup!'

Kian and Shane became friends when they were both about ten, and Mark joined the gang a few years later. 'I was OK at school, but, once I did my Junior Certificate [O levels], all I was interested in was music. Mark and I would sit together during maths class and write songs, then rush out afterwards and show them to Shane. And the rehearsals for the musicals were always after school and I'd be sitting in class, counting the minutes, dying for the bell and four o'clock.'

Kian was mad into music all right, but he was the fussy sort: 'I remember Shane once saying to me, "How about getting a boy band together?" and I just laughed at him. I was a rocker when I was about twelve. I had long hair, played guitar and loved bands like Metallica, Guns N' Roses and Bon Jovi.'

But Kian realised that this was not the path to *Top of the Pops* when he was beaten in a school talent contest – by his own brother. 'My rock band Pyromania used to enter the contest every year, and we'd always come second to my brother Tom's band, Fiction – they only won because they nicked the song that we planned to do!' (Not a sore loser, by any chance, Kian?)

A big moment for Kian was when he and his gang headed to Dublin to see one of their heroes, Michael Jackson, who was on his spectacular HIStory tour. 'It was the first concert I ever saw – we all went up – me, Shane, Mark, Graham and my cousin Michael. We were blown away by the show! Michael Jackson shouted, "I love you, Dublin" from the stage. We were all cheering madly, even though we were from Sligo! Shane was such a fan that he took a clump of grass home with him from the venue. We kept touching the grass all the way home.'

As stars of so many local musicals, Kian and his pals were starting to get a following of their own, and began to dream about a pop career. 'After school, we'd all go to Graham's house and watch Take That and Backstreet Boys videos and we decided we wanted to do the same thing.'

Then Six as One/IO YOU formed. 'We practised everywhere — in one of the local community centres and also in Shane's café because the acoustics were good there. We'd record ourselves in rehearsals; we'd watch videos of other bands. School work was going to the dogs, and our parents were all going crazy.'

But then Shane's mum changed everything . . .

Nicky

It's not unusual for a son to follow his dad into the family business — but it's a bit different when your father is in showbiz, as Nicky discovered. 'It's no wonder I've been singing all my life, as my dad is in a band called Nikki and the Studs. I'd sometimes go to gigs with him and watch him set up the gear and listen to the audiences getting into the show. I suppose I was learning about the business without realising it. My dad's a lead singer, and I always wanted to be one, too, although I was too shy to get up on a stage.' However, the desire to entertain a crowd was definitely in Nicky's blood — his first live performance was at the age of four, when he took centre stage at his auntie's wedding to sing 'Karma Chameleon'. But, after that, football took over — until a TV show changed his life one fateful night. 'I was about twelve or thirteen when Boyzone started, and one night they sang on the Irish TV chat show, *The Late Late Show*. I remember they were wearing orange jumpsuits. My sister had taped them, and I started watching the video with some of my mates. I was slagging off the band to the lads, going, "Look at the state of them. What a sad bunch!" But deep down I thought they were absolutely amazing. I loved the band and wanted to be a part of it. But I didn't tell any of my mates that I was a Boyzone fan, because I knew they would think I was going soft.'

But you can't deny your destiny, no matter how hard you try. Even when he moved to Leeds, Nicky couldn't get Boyzone out of his mind. 'I confessed up to being a fan, and, while the other Leeds lads would be playing dance music, I'd be listening to my Boyzone records — one of the lads on the team even nicknamed me Ronan!'

When he returned from Leeds, Nicky decided to try to break into the music business; but first, he took his Leaving Certificate at Plunkett College in Whitehall in Dublin. His English teacher, Deirdre McCartan, remembers him well: 'He was always singing — he would even serenade the teachers in and out of the classroom! Even then, Ronan Keating was his idol, and once he confessed to me that he didn't have time to finish an essay because he had to go up to the local shopping centre to get the new Boyzone record! And he wrote an essay for his Christmas test, in which he described how one day he'd be in a famous pop band. I seem to remember laughing at him at the time. I hope I don't bump into him now!'

But Nicky was determined. With some of the money he had saved from his time in Leeds, he and his dad went out and bought a karaoke machine and loads of discs. 'I went around to my girlfriend's house and spent until five in the morning on her computer, typing out songs for our new act, "Father and Son Karaoke". I got loads of cards printed up, and dropped them in pubs all around Dublin. Karaoke was huge at the time — I was singing in karaoke competitions. I got to the final of one by dressing up in a suit like Ronan and by singing like him. But I knew that if I wanted to succeed, I would have to develop my own style.'

Bryan

Not even the wildest pack of horses in the world could drag Bryan off a stage. He loves it, and is happiest when singing and dancing in front of a crowd. Bryan learned a lot with the Billie Barry Stage School — Edele and Keavy from B*Witched were pupils there, as was Mikey from Boyzone — and started to get more interested in dancing.

'As I got a bit older, I started to worry about my weight, and I found that dancing was a great way to shed a few pounds. Suddenly, my nights started getting busier — in any one week, I'd be doing football training, hip-hop dancing three nights a week, then I'd have a show on Saturday and a football match on Sunday. And I was going to a gym. It was all go.'

Bryan stayed with Billie Barry until he was seventeen, doing shows – and he even got a part in an Irish TV series, *Finbarr's Class* – but then felt the tug of other types of music.

'I wanted to do something more acceptable to my age, and I started hip-hop dancing. There were about fifty or sixty of us and it was a brilliant buzz. But, after I had to turn down a TV appearance with the dance troupe because I was doing a Billie Barry show in the Point theatre the same evening, I knew I had to choose between them.'

Then, at Christmas 1997, he and two of the guys he danced with, Darragh Deane and Tim Madigan, got up on stage during a karaoke night and sang a Backstreet Boys' song. 'Everyone thought we sounded great together, so we started a band, called Cartel.'

The band clicked right away. 'We built up a following really quickly, and played loads of gigs around Dublin. We sang mainly a *cappella* and girls loved us! I was also learning loads about the music business. We had a manager for a while, but I was also beginning to find out about how to book gigs, about how to record songs, about how to get on the radio.'

About this time, Bryan started to contact Irish record companies in the hope of getting a record deal for Cartel. 'I got a list of the various companies, and I'd ring around as many as I could, and talked the ears off anyone who picked up the phone!'

One of the numbers that Bryan acquired along the way was that of the famous Boyzone manager, Louis Walsh. 'I eventually got him on the line, and I waffled on and on for about an hour about the band and anything else I could think of! When he finally managed to get a word in edgeways, he said, "I'm not looking for a whole new band: I'm just looking for one person to put in the line-up of a new band, IO YOU. Send me a picture and a tape of Cartel, and I'll have a listen." Naturally, I put them in the post the next day. But he never got them . . .'

3 The Birth of the Band — And Then There Were Five

Louis Walsh lives in a lovely, spacious apartment on a quiet, leafy road in Dublin. Or it would be a spacious apartment if it weren't for the mountainous piles of CDs, video cassettes, tapes, photographs and letters that take up almost every inch of space. And this is just the stuff he brings home from his office!

And goodness only knows when he has time to wade through it all, because, every sixty seconds, one of his two phones starts to ring. In 1998, it was very difficult to get hold of the live-wire music manager, who truly sits still only when he's strapped into a plane seat during take-off. For he was a very busy man — his band Boyzone were one of the biggest pop acts in the world, and every wannabe star wanted a touch of his magic.

Mae Filan was no different from the dozens of mothers who contacted Louis to tell him about their talented child — but Mae had one big advantage. She came from the same place as Louis, the wee town of Kiltimagh in County Mayo, which is so far west that the next piece of dry land is Manhattan Island.

'He'd seen us on a TV news show, when we went to the local hospital to sing to the sick children,' explains Shane. 'It turned out that he was looking for us – but he wasn't looking particularly hard, and he may never have made contact if my mum hadn't rung him first.'

Louis agreed to meet the Sligo lads, and suggested that they call into the POD nightclub in Dublin that evening.

Shane says, 'We didn't know what to expect. I sort of thought that he'd look like a cool rocker – all long hair, leather jacket and earrings. Instead, he just looked like an ordinary guy!'

'We just stood there for about half an hour,' says Kian, 'and he gave us advice about contracts, and he offered to sort us out with a manager, because he didn't want to take on a second boy band. And then, at the end of the night, he just turned around and said, "Why don't we put you supporting Boyzone at Christmas?" We were totally gobsmacked!'

Shane and Michael got another glimpse of pop stardom when Louis invited them to Ronan Keating's 21st-birthday party at the Red Box, a music venue above the POD, on 3 March. After this, the boys returned to Sligo in triumph. To celebrate their unbelievable piece of good luck, the band gathered in the local pub. It was a weekend night, and everyone was relaxed and happy. Then Shane's mother rang the pub. Louis had just called her and asked if IO YOU would be interested in supporting the Backstreet Boys in Dublin the following Tuesday night.

Would they? You bet they would!

'We were in shock,' says Kian. 'I was running around the

room like a lunatic. Graham actually fell on his knees crying, and Shane was freaking out: "What'll we wear? What songs will we sing?"'

And so the lads got their first taste of fame and screaming girls – and Kian loved it.

'We were walking into the venue,' he says, 'and all these girls started running towards us and screaming! We were all looking at each other, going, "Why are they screaming at us? We're nobodies!" The girls were roaring, "Are ye the dancers?" and we all started shouting back, "No – we're better than that. We're the support band!" '

'It was unreal,' says Shane. 'We watched the Backstreet Boys rehearse, and we were in awe. We ended up playing basketball with their Nick and their Brian, which was weird, given what was to happen in our band.'

And then IO YOU stepped on to their biggest-ever stage. 'I'd never seen such a crowd in my life as when I walked out on to that stage,' says Mark. 'There could have been twenty million people out there, for all I could tell. The sea of faces went on for ever. And the noise was like a wave hitting you between the eyes. Before we went on, I was like jelly in the wings, but the crowd just lifted me up, and I went for it.

'We used to get a buzz out of playing in front of two hundred people in a nightclub, so this was the buzz multiplied by infinity. I can't describe the feeling of excitement inside me. I just lost it on stage and started jumping up and down. I didn't care what I looked like – though when I saw the video afterwards I thought we all looked like a bunch of Munchkins!'

But Louis was on hand to bring the six ecstatic lads back down to earth with a loud bump: 'We all piled off the stage and were gathered around Louis going, "What did you think?" and he said, "It was good, guys." We stood there, going, "What do you mean it was good? We were brilliant! We heard the crowd screaming for us!" And then, after the second show, he dropped the bombshell . . .'

Louis called Kian into a room. 'Louis said to me, "OK, this is the story. I want to manage you. But six is too many. If you want me to manage the band, you'll have to cut the numbers down." '

The band returned to Sligo to think things over. 'It suddenly wasn't a joke any more. Louis changed everything,' says Mark. 'He suddenly started talking about record deals and songwriters. He said that six was too many, so the band had a meeting, and we agreed that everyone had to try their very best, and if anyone had to leave, then the rest of us would have to live with the decision.'

Derek Lacey was the first to be axed, and the band told him a few days later. It was no fun: 'I don't get upset easily,' says Mark, 'but it was horrible telling Derek, because you could see the excitement on his face as much as anyone else in the band. If it had been me, I would have been totally gutted. We had started out as six fellas having a laugh, and then it grew and grew, and people were being left behind. It felt like being on an aeroplane with six engines, setting off on a big adventure, and then one of the engines just blew up.'

The dust settled, but only for a short while. IO YOU started rehearsing for a series of live outdoor touring shows run by the Irish broadcasting organisation RTE called the Beat on the Street. They got their first choreographer, Jane Shortall, and travelled to London to record two tracks, 'Everybody Knows' and 'Good Thing' with the top song-writer/producer Steve Mac. Then the axe fell for the second time . . .

'When we came back from London, Louis took me aside and said that Graham wasn't right for the band,' says Kian. 'I was absolutely horrified, as he was my best friend in the world. I just couldn't tell him. I couldn't do it.' In the end, Louis rang Graham, but persuaded him to stay on as the band's tour manager.

So then there were four. As fate would have it — and fate plays a big part in the Westlife story — another music pro-moter, Noel Carty, had dreamed up a new idea. He wanted to put together an Irish traditional boy band — Boyzone meets the Dubliners. He set up an audition for Saturday 19 June in the Red Box, advertised in the papers, and enlisted the help of several experts to help him choose — including Ray Hedges and Louis Walsh.

One person who spotted the audition notice in the paper was an aunt of Nicky's girlfriend, Georgina. This was the big chance that Nicky had been waiting for, so he sprang into action straightaway. 'I set up my karaoke machine in the house, recorded some songs and went to a modelling agency and got some professional pictures taken. I sent the tape and photos off, and got a letter back, inviting me to the auditions.'

But the local grapevine was also hard at work. One

morning, Bryan popped into a hair salon to get a quick trim, and got chatting to the stylist. 'Later the stylist rang me and said that he had recommended me to his pal, Louis Walsh, who wanted me to go to the audition,' says Bryan.

Nicky took the train into the city that Saturday morning, all spiffed up in his best suit. He thought he'd get to the venue in plenty of time – the early songbird gets the worm. But, unfortunately for him, everyone else had the same idea.

'There was a queue of about three hundred ahead of me. I thought to myself, Oh, God, am I going to even make it inside the door? I was afraid they were going to take in the first hundred, and tell everyone else to get lost. I really wanted to get in so badly. I was walking to the end of the queue, passing every type of fella you could think of. Blokes with long hair and guitars, blokes with short hair and woolly jumpers. Guys who looked like Ronan, or Shane Lynch or Gary Barlow.'

Then he had his first stroke of luck – he saw a lad he knew close to the top of the queue, who called him over. 'It was brilliant, he was about six from the front, so I skipped loads of places.'

Then he had his second piece of luck: 'The organiser went down the queue telling us that we could sing either "Father and Son" or the ballad "She Moved Through the Fair". I knew both songs off by heart, and had actually sung the ballad as part of my Junior Cert exam. So I picked "Father and Son". '

And luck always comes in threes . . . 'I was looking at the other guys in the queue, and I spotted this guy who looked familiar, but I couldn't place from where. He looked too cool for a boy band! He was dressed in street gear — baggy bottoms and a baseball cap. So I just started talking to him. He introduced himself as Bryan.'

Bryan had turned up full of hope — he too got a lucky break. He spotted a TV camera crew covering the auditions, and one of the crew was a neighbour, who slipped Bryan into the venue at the head of the queue. 'I thought I had a good chance, but I wasn't overconfident,' says Bryan. 'I was looking around me and thinking, There's no way some of these lads could be in a boy band. I went in my Tommy Hillfiger bottoms and a baseball cap, and looked like someone who was in a band. Most of the rest were in dodgy-looking jeans and shirts, or suits.

'Then I saw Nicky and just started chatting to him. He was the only person I talked to during the audition, funnily enough.'

But Nicky's good luck almost ran out on him when he took his place on the stage. 'It was very intimidating. There was a long table in front of the stage with loads of people at it, and hundreds of other hopefuls milling about, watching. I just thought to myself, Now, Nicky, sing your heart out! Sing! But I started singing too early, and was totally out of time with the backing track! I thought I'd blown it, but then I saw Ray Hedges gesturing at the engineer to stop the tape, so I just kept on going.'

Bryan was also one of the first on. 'I wanted to sing my own songs, and I wasn't sure of the words to the Boyzone songs, but I sort of made them up as I went along.'

Nicky was hanging around, wondering what to do, when

a security guard tapped him and said that Louis Walsh wanted to meet him. 'I went over and Louis started asking me loads of questions. Then he said, "I'm starting a pop band and you could be in it. I'd like you to meet one of the lads." I thought he said he was starting a "pub band", and I didn't want to join a pub band! But then he introduced me to Kian, who was wearing a tight top, baggy jeans and was dripping in jewellery and who was definitely in a pop band!'

Kian was working with Louis to find a fifth member for the band. 'I was firing off all these questions at the lads, like, "Would you leave your girlfriend for the band?" I even asked Nicky that! He looked at me as if I was mad! But I thought I was really cool.'

Nicky and Bryan ended up singing together that evening for the very first time, at Nicky's karaoke night in a pub in Malahide on the north side of Dublin. And both of them got a call back for the final audition in the same venue on the following weekend.

'There were about thirty guys in the room,' says Nicky, 'and Louis said, "Who wants to go first?" and of course Bryan was up onstage like a shot! I was gutted, because he sang so well!'

Then it was Nicky's turn. He sang 'Words'. 'I didn't think I sang that well, but next thing the numbers in the room were down to ten, then five, then three. And then it was just Bryan and me.'

Then the lads had to do a dance audition.

'Dancing wasn't me at all,' Nicky confesses. 'I was in a suit as well, while Bryan was dressed really funkily. I wasn't happy with that at all!'

Bryan, on the other hand, was well happy: 'I was thinking, Yesss! I knew NIcky was a footballer and so couldn't dance to save his life! He tied himself up in knots and I was thinking, Brownie points for me!'

As it happened, none of the Sligo boys could choose between Nicky and Bryan. They were both perfect. But Louis was adamant that the new band could have only five members, and IO YOU were already four — Kian, Mark, Shane and Michael.

And time was running out. A&R people from all the major record companies were flying into Dublin to hear the band play. So the four Sligo lads and the two Dubs went to Sligo to rehearse and to try to choose between one of the two newcomers — even the media picked up on the dilemma, with one paper running a picture of the rivals under a headline, 'THE BATTLE OF THE BLONDES'!

On the day of their first big showcase with Virgin, the band gathered together. Louis told a couple of the Sligo boys, 'It's decision time. Nicky and Bryan are perfect. I think Michael is wrong for the band. But I'll leave the decision up to you. But you must decide now.'

Another agonised meeting. But everyone in his heart knew that with Bryan and Nicky the new band would be something really special. A band good enough to take on the world.

'In the end, Graham was the only one with the courage to tell Michael,' says Kian. 'He called us all together, and then Graham said, "Right. IO YOU are now Shane, Mark, Kian, Bryan — and Nicky. I'm sorry, Michael.'

It was a strange feeling for the boys. They were thrilled for themselves, but also felt terrible about Michael, who sat in tears in the room, his dreams cruelly turned to dust. But Nicky felt for him, even through his own happiness: 'After a while, I went over to Michael. I didn't know what to say to him as it was me and Bryan who had taken his place. So I just said, "I know I'm the last person you want to talk to, but I just wanted to tell you that last summer when I was let go from Leeds it felt like the end of the world. Football was my life, but I bounced back. You'll bounce back too." '

But now, through a combination of phone calls and fate, the line-up was complete. To mark their new look, IO YOU became Westside – before it was discovered that another band already has the name, and it was then quickly changed to Westlife – and Nicky's hero, Ronan Keating, became their co-manager. And on 20 October 1998, the final piece of the puzzle fell into place when they signed a massive £4 million record deal with RCA.

'We had talked to lots of different record companies,' says Shane. 'But, as soon as Simon Cowell of RCA walked in, it was different. We were less than two minutes into our showcase, when he turned to Louis and said, "I want to sign this band now," and then started talking to us about working with various writers and producers, and we both wanted exactly the same thing. We knew that, with Simon on board with Louis and Ronan, we had the perfect team. But none of us in our wildest dreams could have guessed just how fast everything was going to change for us . . .'

Profile: Mark

FULL NAME:	**Marcus Michael Patrick Feehily**
DATE OF BIRTH:	**28 May 1980**
STAR SIGN:	**Gemini**
MUM AND DAD:	**Marie and Oliver**
BROTHERS/SISTERS:	**Barry and Colin**
HEIGHT:	**5 ft 10 in**
COLOUR OF EYES:	**Blue**
ANY SCARS OR TATTOOS?	**A birthmark on my back, and a big dent of a scar on my right shin, and some scars on my hand from glass cuts**

What do the rest of Westlife think of Mark?

Kian: Mark is very funny – you can be in tears laughing at Mark if he's in the right mood. But he likes to spend time on his own, chilling out in his room watching TV, or going for a long walk.

Shane: He's very quiet, and can be very shy until you get to know him. He likes his privacy, but is a totally genuine guy, with no bull about him. And he loves singing – he sings all day. He's got such a brilliant voice.

Nicky: Mark is very laid back. He's quiet until you get to know him, then he can be quite mad! He's a really cool guy, and nothing bothers him unless he's overtired! He's a really cool guy and very talented. I love his voice – I'd kill for a voice like his!

Bryan: He likes to do his own thing, and he's always giving our tour manager, Anto, heart attacks, because he's so good at disappearing into a crowd! But he loves music and has an amazing voice. Mark is the tall, dark, sensitive one in the band. He can be quite shy, but he is affectionate and funny once he decides that you're his friend. He's a bit of a home bird, and his friends and family in Sligo are very important to him — which is why he always seems to have a phone growing out of his ear! One of his pet hates is morning time, and it takes him a while to get going if the band have an early start. But he usually manages to catch up on a few Zs in the back of the van, on the plane, skiing down the side of Mount Everest — only joking! He loves singing in the shower, and is a huge fan of singers like Left Eye from TLC and Mariah Carey . . .

Mark in his own words

My dream home: It would be close to Sligo, but right beside water, either a lake or the sea as I'd like a jet ski. I'd have a big party area with a bar and a snooker table. I'd have a massive TV and hundreds of computer games — I'll be a kid all my life!

My earliest memory: I remember being on a family holiday in Wales, when I was about three. I was left asleep in my cot while the adults went downstairs to have dinner in the hotel restaurant. But I woke up and climbed out of the cot — I was in a panic, because I thought Mum and Dad had gone back to Ireland without me! I couldn't reach the doorknob, so I got the wastepaper bin from the bathroom, emptied it on the floor and climbed up on it so I could open the door. My parents couldn't believe it when I toddled into the restaurant on my own!

My first kiss: I was about twelve, and she was an exchange student I met at a house party organised by a friend's parents. The kiss was a serious shock for the first minute, but after a little while I began to enjoy it! I've never looked back since . . .

My ideal girl: She would have to have a good sense of humour, as I'm always cracking jokes. Most of my jokes are sarcastic, so she'd have to be well able to answer me back! I don't like girls who are plastered in make up I like it if they look good in casual clothes, like a tracksuit. And I also like a girl who doesn't get too intense about a relationship after just a few weeks. But at the moment I'm just into having a laugh. I like going to nightclubs and chatting up girls, and maybe have a dance and a smooch. Some people try too hard to find someone special, but I believe if it's meant to happen to me, it will someday.

Q&A
Who is your best friend in the band?
All of them are *soooo* cool – I can't choose between them!
Are you a morning person or a night owl?
Night owl – I detest mornings!
Do you read your horoscope?
Yes.

Do you believe in aliens? If so, what do you imagine they look like?

Yes. I've never seen one, but I know they're out there!

What was the first record you ever bought?

Michael Jackson's 'Bad'.

How useful are you in the kitchen? What can you rustle up if you have to?

I'm pretty good. I can cook chicken and fried rice, steak and chips, beans on toast, lasagne, apple tart, tea and toast, etc., etc.

What part of your body would you change, if you could (keep it clean, lads)?

Emm – my left little toe!

Would you consider cosmetic surgery?

No way!

Are you ticklish? If so, where (careful now)?

Not really. I suppose maybe down below – my feet, I mean!

What is the most expensive thing you've ever bought?

A laptop computer.

What is the most useless thing you've ever bought?

A laptop computer! Ah, no, really it was a map of America.

What is the worst present you've ever received?

I received nothing once!

Have you ever been in hospital?

Yes – I swallowed all my granny's tablets and had to get my stomach pumped. (Gimme a break – I was three years old!)

What is your favourite breakfast?

Beans, rasher, sausage, black and white pudding – but no egg!

Hangover cures – what is the most effective?

Not drinking too much!

If you went on a blind date, who would you most like to find sitting on the bar stool?

Mariah, Shaznay, Billie, Britney, Louise Nurding . . . the list goes on . . .

Have you ever written poetry?

A wee bit – I write more song lyrics than poetry.

What is your favourite TV programme?

Friends, South Park, Ali G, MTV Select – I can be a bit of a couch potato!

What is your favourite item of clothing?

I love baggy bottoms, big warm hoodies and runners (trainers).

What is your most embarrassing item of clothing?

A brutal pair of white shoes I had to wear for the Party in the Park in London last July.

What scares the living daylights out of you?

The thought of anything happening to my loved ones.

What is the last thing you lost?

My passport.

What is your favourite smoochy record?

Recently, I've been sticking on Toni Braxton's new album.

You've recorded with Mariah – who's next for a duet (or sextet, whatever)?

I'd love to work with Michael Jackson.

Who is your favourite musician/actor/actress?

Stevie Wonder, Eddie Murphy, Lisa Kudrow (Phoebe from *Friends*).

What are the best films you have ever seen?

The best were *Armageddon* and *The Green Mile*. The worst was *Bowfinger*.

Westlife: In Real Life

What is the best book you have ever read?
Angela's Ashes by Frank McCourt.
Are you superstitious?
Yes – I can be a bit stupid about it sometimes.
Did you enjoy school? What was your favourite subject?
They were the best days of my life – I loved French.
What false names have you used in the past when checking into a hotel?
Emm – Mr Black, Mr Murphy, Mr Magoo!
Do you have a lucky charm? If so, what is it?
Yes, it's actually . . . I'm not gonna say!
Are you romantic?
I can be – it depends on the atmosphere!
Have you ever had your heart broken? If so, when, and by whom?
Yes, when I was younger. It was puppy love!
How old were you when you had your first kiss? Did you enjoy it?
I was twelve or thirteen – it was horrible for the first minute, then it was nice!
Where is your favourite place in the world?
Sligo, Ireland, by far!
Do you sing in the shower?
Oh, yeah – you can't stop me!
Do you lose your temper easily?
No – I'm very calm and collected.
Do you cry easily?
No – it takes a lot to make me cry.

What is the worst job you ever had?
Cleaning toilets in a fast-food place!
What is your favourite sport to watch and/or play?
I love watching football, and playing tennis, squash and football.
If you weren't in a band, what do you think you'd be up to?
Maybe teaching French, or a I'd be a social worker or doing something with computers.
What do you imagine your life will be like in ten years' time?
I can't guess – as long as myself, my family and friends have our happiness and our health, I'll be delighted!

4 The Westlife Wonderteam

Shane, Nicky, Mark, Bryan and Kian have all been perfect since birth. Each of them grew up knowing how to sing like an angel and dance like Michael Jackson. They never, ever wore dodgy jumpers or sported pudding bowl haircuts. And, of course, they all know everything about the music business: how to make hit records, write hit songs, how to get on MTV and how to get from Melbourne to Kuala Lumpur without losing any members of the band.

True? Nah – if a band like that ever shows up, the rest of the pop world can all go home. While Westlife are gifted with special singing talents and a fierce determination to be the biggest, coolest band in the universe, they couldn't do it all on their own.

The secret of their success lies also in the Westlife Wonderteam – the people who have helped to launch the band, who look after them on their mad adventures around the world, who write and produce their beautiful ballads and who help them avoid fashion disasters and falling over their own feet on stage. These are the faces who take Westlife places.

Louis Walsh: Pop Manager

Louis Walsh is living proof that the scientists have got it wrong — lightning does strike twice in the same place. When Louis launched Boyzone in Ireland at the end of 1993, everyone thought he was mad. 'I had tried everything else, to be honest,' he admits. 'So I just decided to try a Take That style of band.'

And, 12 million album sales later, even Louis's biggest critics were forced to admit that it hadn't been such a mad idea after all. And in 1998, when Louis decided to search for a second boy band, the entire pop business sat up and took notice, especially Shane Filan and Kian Egan. 'When the two lads called to see me in the POD, I really liked them as people — although I thought they looked like a pair of culchies! I was looking for another band, as I knew time was running out for Boyzone, and I wanted a band full of great vocalists, like Boys II Men.'

Louis reckons that signing with RCA Records was the band's biggest break. 'Simon Cowell in RCA has been really supportive of the band from the start. We showcased for loads of companies, but no one offered us the sort of deal we wanted, until Simon came along. In fact, I still ring some of the other record companies, every time that Westlife go to Number One, just to remind them.'

Westlife's manager is the first to agree that the band work unbelievably hard: 'They have a great attitude, which I love about them. They are prepared to work very, very hard to be successful, and they know there's a big price to pay. In a band like Westlife, you don't have a normal life — the boys are on call twenty-four hours a day, to do interviews, TV appearances, to meet the fans, hop on planes. If bands don't work hard, they're no use to me.'

Although he gets on brilliantly with the boys, as the Boss, Louis isn't afraid to crack the whip: 'They're very dedicated, but if they start moaning about doing something I just say to them, "Shut up — you could be playing in Strandhill [a small village outside Sligo] tonight!" I always choose one band member to ring to pass on messages, and in Westlife it's Kian. I shout and scream at him if the band are terrible on TV, or if they're not looking well, or if I hear they've been out too late!'

But, then, Louis works just as hard himself. A fizzing bundle of energy, he is famous in the music industry for the long hours he puts in every day, looking after his various acts — he manages Westlife, Ronan Keating, Samantha Mumba and the new Irish girl band, Bellefire. He has three phones, home, mobile and office, which ring around the clock — it's not unusual to ring Louis and hear splashing sounds in the background. Yes, he even takes his phone into the bath!

'I don't travel with the band when they're away. My job is to get on the phone — first, to make sure that everyone else is working! Then it's about finding songs, talking to producers, video makers, TV people, dealing with the press. My phones ring all the time, from eleven in the morning to eleven at night. Luckily for me, I love the music business.'

If you are ever standing beside Louis, you will hear a typical phone call. His mobile rings . . . 'Hello? . . . That's me . . . Yes, yes, yes . . . OK, OK, OK. Bye-bye, bye-bye, bye-bye.'

Or you could ask one of the boys from Westlife: they all do wicked Impressions of their boss in action!

Simon Cowell: A&R Consultant

Simon Cowell can change people's lives with the stroke of a pen! He has worked in A&R — which stands for Artiste & Repertoire — for twenty years. The A&R person has one of the most important jobs in a record company: it involves spotting young, unknown bands, figuring out whether they are going to be famous or flops — and, if it's the first, signing them before rival record companies start sniffing around! The A&R department then works with the newly signed band, helping to shape their sound and their style.

At the moment, Simon is working with Westlife, Five and Girl Thing. He signed Robson and Jerome, and also — oh, dear! — passed on a chance to sign another bunch of young chaps: Boyzone. So, when Louis came calling a second time, Simon was quick to check out his new boys — but it took a little persuading . . .

'Louis rang me and asked if I would have a look at his new band, IO YOU,' says Simon. 'So I flew to Dublin and met them in a hotel and heard them sing.' At this stage, IO YOU were Mark, Shane, Kian, Graham, Michael and Derek. But Simon was interested in only two of the lads, Mark and Kian.

'Louis played a very sneaky trick on me,' explains Simon. 'He knew that Shane had real talent, and wanted to keep him in the band, so he got Shane to change the colour and style of his hair, and got him some new clothes. When I came back three months later to see the band again, I didn't recognise him and thought he was a new guy!'

This time, when Simon saw the new line-up with Nicky and Bryan, he didn't hesitate. Two minutes into the showcase, he turned to Louis and said, 'I want to sign the band.' He took to them immediately: 'We sat down and had a coffee, and the boys were asking me a million questions about recording and songs. I thought they were really talented.'

And Simon worked hard with the band. He had heard a rumour that the top songwriters Steve Mac and Wayne Hector had a fantastic tune which they had written for another act. 'I invited the writers into my office, and basically locked the door and refused to let them out until they agreed to give Westlife the song! It was called "Flying Without Wings". ' And, after the song was recorded, it was Simon who suggested that a gospel choir might sound quite good on the track! Nice one, Simon . . .

Anto Byrne: Tour Manager

So you're in Singapore. You've had three hours' sleep, its 95 degrees in the shade, there are two thousand fans screaming outside the hotel, and you were supposed to be downstairs ten minutes ago to leave for the airport. Trouble is, you can't find your passport. So what do you do? You call Anto.

The band are the first to admit that chaos would reign without Anto to keep the whole Westlife circus rolling smoothly from one city to the next. For it's almost impossible to describe what Anto Byrne's job is all about: he co-ordinates their tour schedules, books hotels and flights, gets

The guys with Anto Byrne, their tour manager, at Party in the Park 2000

them up and running in the mornings, ensures their luggage hasn't gone astray, organises security, sorts out all the band's various problems, deals with the record companies and replaces lost mobile phones (which happens a lot!) He's even been known to cook the odd meal for the guys if he thinks they're overdosing on fast food!

Anto has worked with loads of Irish artists, including Van Morrison, and Louis Walsh describes him as 'the best in the business'. And, in a weird way, Anto was destined to work with Westlife, as there are some strange coincidences between him and Nicky.

Anto explains, 'We both have four-inch-long scars on the same elbow; we both have scars on our bellies; we both have one brother and one sister; both our dads are painters and decorators; and we both have aunties living in Toronto, Canada, who worked together in the same office!'

And Anto vividly remembers the first time he met the band. 'Louis called me and said he had a band that he'd like me to work with. So he gave me Kian's number. I rang him, and went down to the Red Box to meet them all.'

At first, they were a bit wary of Anto, as he was taking over their friend Graham's job as tour manager.

'They asked me what artists I had worked with, and I named Van Morrison. And they all went, "Who's he?" They weren't impressed! But then I mentioned that I'd just returned that same morning from Japan, where I'd been touring with a band called the Hothouse Flowers. Suddenly they were firing questions at me, asking what it's like to be on the road, and what sort of tour bus they were going to get. So I reckoned I had the job.'

Although they all got on fantastically well from the start, Anto had one little problem: 'It took me a little while to learn their names! I used to carry a little flyer of the band – which had their names beside their pictures – around in my wallet. I'd sneak the flyer out of my wallet, match the face to the picture, then bark at whoever it was!'

But, travelling with the band, he soon learned all their funny little ways – especially in the early mornings. 'Nicky's always up first thing, but I have to ring Shane two or three times, and sometimes I have to ring Mark on his hotel phone and his mobile at the same time to get him moving. They'll all fall out of the lift two minutes before we have to leave, and then, half an hour down the road, they're all howling at me to stop for breakfast. And they have to eat – they get really grumpy when they're hungry. Especially Nicky "I Need A Meal" Byrne!'

Poor Anto – it's worse than having a bunch of kids, really.

Pete Waterman: Producer and Songwriter

In 1988, when eight-year-old Bryan and ten-year-old Nicky bought their first-ever record – 'I Should Be So Lucky' by Kylie Minogue – neither boy could have guessed that a decade later one of Kylie's legendary producers would be working with them.

Just as the 1990s pop charts were dominated by boy bands and gal groups, the legendary trio of Mike Stock, Matt Aitken and Pete Waterman ruled the 1980s, churning out over 130 hit singles for artists such as Kylie, Jason Donovan and Rick Astley.

And in 1999 Pete Waterman landed back at the top of the charts with a bang with Steps' number-one single,

'Tragedy/Heartbeat'. By this time, he had also met the boys from Westlife, who would give Pete a very special Christmas present in December of that year . . .

'I first heard Westlife's voices when my friend Simon Cowell at RCA played me their first single, "Swear It Again". I think I was more excited by their voices than he was! People tend to underestimate the power of the human voice, and to find five very unique and different voices is outstanding. For me, it was like finding at least three Rick Astley's in the same band!'

In May 1999, the band were in Pete's London studio, PWL, to record what would be their Christmas release, 'Seasons In the Sun' and 'I Have a Dream'. As soon as Pete heard 'I Have a Dream', he knew he was on to a winner.

'I rang up a betting shop and asked the bookie what odds he would give me for having my name on the label of the Christmas Number One — I knew that Steps were going to be huge as well, so I was hedging my bet! The bookie was a bit surprised, as it was still only May! But he said, "I'll give you fifteen to one, mate." So I stuck on a thousand pounds. I wasn't even worried when Cliff Richard took Number One in December. I was sure Westlife would do it.'

Also that same week, Pete watched the boys celebrate in his studio when they heard that 'Swear It Again' had gone to Number One in Britain. 'When they heard the news, they went barmy! That's why my job is so fantastic. You can't buy the looks on their faces: it was like someone had dropped them in the biggest sweet shop in the world, and said "take what you like". '

And Pete believes that Westlife will be winners for years to come. 'They could be around for longer than any other band. They're exceptionally talented, and also, being Irish, they have their feet firmly on the ground.' And so say all of us, Pete!

Andrew Berkowitz: Artist Relations in America

America is one of the few places left in the world where Westlife can walk down city streets without being mobbed by girls! But that is all set to change during 2001 – it's just that, with a population of 255 million, you have to shout just a little bit louder to be heard in America.

And that is the job of Andrew Berkowitz, who works for Arista, the band's American record label, in New York. Andrew sets up interviews for bands with radio stations and the all-important TV stations such as MTV. He also travels with the bands when they're doing promotional tours.

Andrew has worked with Five, TLC, Take That and Toni Braxton – but you get the sneaking feeling that Westlife are his favourite act.

'I first met them when they were in New York doing some publicity. It was their first time in America, and they were a bit overwhelmed by it all. I ended up sitting in McDonald's with Kian, Nicky and Shane and then we went down to the Virgin Megastore, as the boys wanted to buy videos of Backstreet Boys and 'N Sync. I thought it was great that they were fans of other groups!'

Every time the band visits the US on promotional tours,

Andrew travels with them (lucky dog), and he got to know all their pet hates. 'Nicky is afraid of lifts, and he won't travel in one on his own,' says Andrew. 'We were in Oklahoma City, and we were all sitting out by the pool – the guys love to work on their tans at every opportunity, 'cos they're so pale! It was very hot, so we decided to go up to our rooms and change into our swimsuits. So I went up in the lift with Nicky, even though our rooms were on different floors. I went to my room, changed and came back down to the pool. A couple of hours passed, and there was no sign of Nicky. Later, when we met up to go to the venue, I asked him what had happened. And he said sadly, "I waited and waited by the lift, but no one came to get me." '

Aah, how sad!

Steve Mac: Producer/Songwriter

Steve Mac was working away in his London studio, Rokstone, when his phone rang. It was Louis Walsh. 'Steve, I've got a band of six guys, and I'd like you to test their voices.'

Steve is one of the most respected writers/producers in the pop business – he had started when he was seventeen, when his first song went to Number Two in the pop charts with a band called Nomad.

So the six members of IO YOU flew to his studio and Steve and his writing partner Wayne Hector spent a Sunday afternoon putting the lads through their paces. 'I kept forgetting their names, but I thought that Shane looked like David Beckham, so I just called him David!'

The next time Steve saw the band, they were Westlife. 'We worked together on the first album, and they were a dream come true for me. Some bands who come into the studio look great but can't sing very well, so Wayne and I have to write simple songs for them. But Westlife could sing anything we gave them – so we gave them "Flying Without Wings", which we wrote in three hours!'

Steve, who also worked in August 2000 with the band on tracks for their second album, believes that Westlife are special: 'I think Westlife are the superstars of pop. Music isn't just a job to them: they love it. And they are fun to work with and very polite – we all keep saying "thank you" to each other all the time!'

Dave Thomas: Stylist

Now, here's a job we'd all hate . . . Imagine having to go around all the top designer stores, borrowing clothes. Imagine having to drop into all the top fashion shows every season to see what colours and clobber are cool. Imagine having to hang around dressing rooms while Westlife run around in their boxers, trying on outfits . . . Hmm, where can we sign up?

The man with more clothes hangers than Marks and Spencer's is Dave Thomas, who has been dressing the fab and famous for twelve years. He has worked with a dizzying number of singers and bands, including Kylie Minogue, Robbie Williams, Oasis, the Corrs, Backstreet Boys and Bon Jovi, and now looks after Westlife as well.

'One of my earlier jobs was changing Kylie's image from

the sweet girl-next-door look into a tougher, sexier look. It was quite dramatic!'

Dave enjoys working with Westlife: 'They're not demanding as people, but the fact that there are five of them gives me lots to do. Sometimes they might have three different photo shoots on the same day, and a TV spot that evening. That means I've got to find twenty different outfits for just one day!'

But at least the band are easier to work with than one particular female superstar whom Dave was styling. 'I was putting together a whole wardrobe for her tour, and she insisted on getting involved in designing all the clothes. But then, the night before the tour started, she decided she hated everything, and it ended up a mad scramble. But I can't tell you who it was.'

MARK AGED TEN, PAINTING A STORAGE TANK –
AND HIMSELF!

SHANE AGED TEN MONTHS

KIAN AT AROUND EIGHTEEN MONTHS

NICKY AGED TWO WITH HIS DAD

BRYAN 'MARRIES' FRIEND WENDY SCANLON, AGED FIVE

BRYAN TAKES TO THE AIR!

WESTLIFE ONSTAGE IN THE USA

THE VIDEO SHOOT FOR THE US RELEASE OF
'SWEAR IT AGAIN' – SHANE GETS A SOAKING!

KIAN, SHANE AND MARK HEAD
OFF TO LONDON FROM IRELAND

BRYAN SNORES
WHILE KIAN
SIGNS
AUTOGRAPHS

A WEEKEND WITH WESTLIFE: PARTY IN THE PARK 2000

ANOTHER WEEKEND WITH WESTLIFE: THE LADS HEAR THEIR NEW SONGS FOR THE FIRST TIME IN STOCKHOLM, SWEDEN

WESTLIFE RECEIVE THE FREEDOM OF SLIGO, JULY 2000

5 On The Road — It's a Mad, Mad, Mad, Mad Westlife World

The early daze . . .

Once the band had signed on the dotted line with RCA, they might have thought they could rest on their laurels for a while — sit back, enjoy the moment and carefully plot out the future.

Boy, were they mistaken! Before the ink on their contract was dry, the band were straight into a whirlwind of touring, TV and radio promotion, recording and video making.

But they had only themselves to blame — no one expected Westlife to take off like a rocket from the very start! After they'd scooped the *Smash Hits* 'Battle of the Bands' Best New Tour Act award in December 1998, the number one hits started to pile up, as did the gold and platinum discs.

It was all a huge adventure, full of First Moments: 'It was amazing to hear our song on the radio for the first time,' recalls Bryan. 'At one stage, I was back in Dublin, sick with glandular fever, while the rest of the lads were touring. They rang me and said, "Listen to this!" and held the phone up to a radio. I could just about hear "Swear It Again" over all the screams on the bus!'

But it wasn't all fun and games on the support tour. Their tour manager Anto made them all pay dearly for being late out of bed in the mornings. 'At the start, there was fierce competition to see who got the front seat of the van beside me, as it was the most comfortable,' says Anto. 'Since we left the hotel at 6.30 a.m. most mornings, whoever wanted the seat would have to be standing by the van by about 6.15 a.m.!' Anto was always happy to see Mark in the front: 'It was brilliant, because he would just sit there and sing all day while he was reading a book or looking out the windows.'

And Anto also operated a strict fines system for stragglers. 'If anyone was late on to the bus, they would have to hand over five pounds out of their daily allowance of fifteen pounds. It doesn't work any more, though!'

Sometimes arguments would break out over which direction Anto should take. 'I'd be driving along and one of the lads would say, "Don't go that way! Turn right, turn right!" – even though he'd never been to England before! He just felt that Birmingham should be over that way.'

Early one particular morning, Westlife were lucky not to lose Anto altogether. It was seven o'clock and the band were on the way to Bristol in the van. Anto was not in a good mood.

'They were mess-fighting in the back of the van – shoving each other around and making a huge racket. My knuckles were white around the steering wheel, doing about sixty-five miles an hour and thinking, Louis, what have you got me into? Next thing, I felt this sudden draught of cold air on my neck.'

Anto looked in his side mirror, and saw Shane's head hanging through a hole where a side window should have been! 'Shane and Mark were tussling, and Mark pushed Shane against a window, which popped out on to the road — and Shane had nearly popped out with it! There were big eighteen-wheeler trucks doing skids behind me and jamming on their brakes.'

It was enough to put the heart crossways on the poor tour manager . . . 'I pulled in sharply, and said, "That's it, lads. I've had enough. I'm going home." I got out of the van and sat on the side of the motorway. All the boys scurried out of the van and said, "We'll go back and get the window." And they walked about half a mile back up the motorway, looking for the pane of glass. Of course they came back with nothing more than a few slivers of broken glass.

'So I just roared, "Get into the van." I was hoarse from shouting by the time we got to Bristol! Then I had to cover the hole with cardboard, and set my alarm to go off every half an hour, so I could get up and check that none of our gear had been stolen out of the van. I got new, black-tinted glass put in the next day. it cost two hundred and eighty pounds — and guess who paid for it!'

But soon the band left the van behind and took to the skies, as the Westlife world domination began. 'Everything happened so fast,' says Shane. 'The success just hit us like a flying brick, and suddenly we were just working, working, working. After "Swear It Again" went to Number One, we were suddenly flying everywhere, from Asia to Europe and then back to Asia. Then "If I Let You Go" went to Number

One, and we were off again. And then we had two Number Ones in six weeks, "Flying Without Wings" and "I Have a Dream". We toured a hundred and four days straight to Christmas Eve without a single day off.

'Just after we signed our deal, we all went out to dinner with Ronan in London, and we were asking him what it was like to be in a big band. And he said, "I'll tell you, lads. It's lots of hard work." And we were going, "Nah – it couldn't be that bad. You're just trying to scare us." '

But it turned out that Ronan was right, as Nicky realised. 'Once, we managed to work in four countries in one day – we woke up in Denmark, then got a bus and a ferry to Sweden, then we flew to Germany and then drove to Holland. Boy, were we confused going to bed that night!'

On another occasion, Nicky got really, really confused. 'We were recording a Christmas special in Poland in 1999, and we'd just arrived in Warsaw from Asia. I was absolutely shattered when I fell into bed. Then I woke up with a jump at about one a.m., and I hadn't a clue where I was. It was dark in the room, and nothing I could see looked familiar. So I just dived on my mobile phone and pressed the redial button. Georgina answered, and I'm shouting down the line. "Where am I? Where am I?" and she was going "Relax – you're in Poland"!'

Flying – with wings

Although flying around the world to new countries may sound like great fun, some of the trips can turn into nightmares, as Westlife found out in summer 2000, when they set off from Asia to America. Andrew Berkowitz from Arista Records recalls the whole sorry tale.

'Last May, the band were flying from Taiwan in the Far East, to Omaha, which is about as far as you can fly in one go. The plane landed in Vancouver in Canada after nineteen hours in the air, but because the flight was late they missed their connection to Omaha. So they flew to Denver in Colorado instead. They arrived in Denver after twenty-four hours' solid flying. At this stage it was after ten p.m., and they couldn't find any hotel rooms. Everything was full. So they rang me.'

Andrew finally found them a motel close to the airport. 'But then it turns out that their luggage had gone on ahead to Omaha, so they had no clean clothes, no toothpaste, no anything. Even Shane, who is normally so unflappable, couldn't even speak down the phone.'

The next morning, the band flew into Omaha, did some promotion work, then took a three-hour flight to Phoenix, Arizona. 'It was a hundred and six degrees, and they were all dressed in heavy clothes,' says Andrew. 'They did a show there, then got on another flight to fly across the Atlantic to Italy to record with Mariah Carey. It was a horror show!'

Two days and one recording session later, the boys were back. 'They came back from Italy to New York,' says Andrew. 'They did the top radio show, *Z100*, then flew to Greensboro in North Carolina in a small plane. When we landed, the runway was in complete darkness as a tornado had just ripped through town and knocked out the electricity. When we got to the hotel, the lifts were out of action so the boys had to haul their very heavy suitcases up six flights of stairs, and there was no hot food anywhere in town. And then, when we got to the theatre for the show, it was cancelled because they never got their electricity back. But all their fans turned up anyway, and the guys stayed until it was pitch dark, and signed every single autograph.'

It's no wonder that sometimes the Westlife boys are a bit slow to climb aboard another plane. Mark, who is famous in the band for his ability to disappear in the middle of a crowded airport, made life very difficult for himself one day in America. 'We were flying from Orlando to Dallas and then on to Springfield in Missouri,' says Anto. 'We were all sitting by the boarding gate, and Mark was on his phone. As we all passed him by on the way to the plane, we were going, "Come on, Mark, it's time to go." But he got up when he was good and ready, strolled to the gate – only to find that the flight was closed and the walkway to the plane had been taken away.' So what does Mark do? He calls Anto . . .

'I'm sitting on the plane, and next thing my phone rings, and it's Mark, saying, "I'm stuck outside and they won't let me on the flight." And I was saying to him, "What exactly do you think I can do about it from seat 2A? Just get to Springfield on time for the show." So he ended up flying from Orlando to Miami to Dallas to Springfield. He still made the show, mind you.'

Given the amount of time that Westlife spend on planes, it was almost inevitable that, the moment the band entered the pop history books, they would be 35,000 feet in the air. And they were. On Sunday 2 April 2000, Westlife became the first group ever to have each of their first five singles enter the UK charts at Number One. It was an incredible moment for the band, who found themselves – almost literally – on Cloud Nine . . . 'We were on a flight to New York when the charts were announced,' says Shane, 'so we had no way of knowing if "Fool Again" had gone to Number One. The suspense was killing us. So Bryan rang Louis from the onboard phone, and Louis said, "You've done it, boys, you've done it. You're Number One again." We all went mad, and started jumping up and down and cheering – that plane rocked for a few minutes, I can tell you. We broke open some champagne, and it never tasted sweeter, and Bryan was yelling, "We're in *The Guinness Book of Records*!" The plane was full of Americans who hadn't a clue who we were and thought we were a bunch of hooligans, but some British people recognised us and started whistling and clapping. But we so wanted to be at home, just for a few hours, to celebrate with our families and friends.'

Kian says, 'We really killed ourselves for that Number One. We worked from 4 a.m. on Friday, right through to 2 a.m.; we did signings everywhere, and satellite links to Manchester and Belfast, and did *TFI Friday*. Then we did the breakfast show on *GMTV*. We were so happy that the fans came through for us on that one.'

Mark says, 'It was brilliant, but there was hardly time to celebrate! We were suddenly on the ground, into the van and off to a video shoot, and we were trying to ring everyone at home at the same time. It was like being given a lump of gold for a few minutes, and then having it snatched away again. There was one report in the papers about us flying five thousand pounds' worth of Guinness to Los Angeles for a celebration party, which was rubbish. I was actually asleep in my bed just after midnight, as we were up at five a.m. the next morning.'

Ah, yes. Sleep. In the past few mad years, Kian, Bryan, Mark, Shane and Nicky have learned to grab shuteye whenever they can.

Kian: 'I can sleep on a nail.'

Shane: 'I can sleep upside down now.'

Nicky: 'I could fall asleep on the side of a coin.'

Bryan: 'I'm always knackered. But I'm usually up for going out!'

And then there's Mark. He's famous for his ability to snatch a few Zs at any opportunity. And even in the most unlikely of places: 'I once fell asleep on a helicopter in Southeast Asia,' he confesses. 'I was so excited about the trip, and I got the front seat, which was on a glass floor. I could see right down to the ground, and we were swooping over amazing scenery, huge forests and jungles. All of a sudden I woke up and we were landing at the hotel! I was kicking myself over that nap!'

Lights . . . cameras . . . action!

In trying to get 'Fool Again' into the record books, the band knew that they had to make a brilliant video to go with the brilliant song. So in early February they took themselves off to Mexico City, to shoot their spectacular mini-movie. 'We love video shoots, because we all love acting,' says Mark. 'It was quite an experience, shooting "Fool Again" in the middle of a city. We were using this big square, and hundreds of locals were ringed around, watching. They had about thirty riot police keeping an eye on things, which was a bit intimidating. But we got to go up on the roof of this really high forty-storey building, and there were helicopters buzzing around filming us. That was great fun.'

According to Bryan, the maddest video shoot they did was when they filmed two on the same day, for their Christmas single, 'I Have a Dream/Seasons in the Sun'. 'That was a crazy day. We were in a big warehouse in London, and it was split into two different sets, one for each video. There were two camera crews, and our costumes were in the middle of the warehouse. So when Mark was on one set doing his solo, we'd all be on the other side singing something else. We were just running between sets, stopping to change on the way. That was a twenty-six-hour day, from 6 a.m. to 8 a.m. the next morning. In the last scene of "I Have a Dream", you can see me falling asleep in the back of the car!'

When West Meets East . . .

Being mobbed by fans is part of the Westlife world now, and for the most part the band love to meet the fans everywhere they go. But nothing could have prepared them for the total madness that greeted them when they travelled around Asia to places such as Malaysia, Indonesia and Singapore.

'We arrived in Indonesia once, and when we came out of the airport there were hundreds of girls being held back by security,' says Nicky. 'It was like that Alfred Hitchcock film,

The Birds. The girls broke through and ran at us, and then it was every man for himself. They were pulling my hair and grabbing at my clothes. I just grabbed my bag of personal stuff and abandoned my suitcase, and I barely made it on to the bus. Eventually, everyone struggled on board, and then the fans started rocking the bus! It was crazy! Then, when we set off, there were about fifty cars following us, driving on both sides of the road and weaving in and out in front of the bus. We all had scrapes on our faces and I had a cross ripped from around my neck.'

The next time the band went back to Indonesia, they brought their own security man, Paul Higgins. Paul is a strong, very experienced security man, but even he had never seen anything like the chaos. 'When we arrived at the airport to fly out, there were about two thousand fans waiting outside the terminal,' says Paul. 'As soon as the van stopped, the fans began rocking it. There was no way out. So I decided to run the lads through the crowd one at a time. I grabbed Bryan and wrestled him through and it took about ten minutes to get him the few yards through the door. Then I had a nightmare trying to get Nicky in. After that, I was wrecked. So the local police jumped into the van and we were able to drive right to the steps of the jumbo. I was black and blue when I woke up the next morning!'

All the band have lost things in the middle of the mad Asian mobs. Kian had a ring pulled from his finger and Nicky was trampled on – but Bryan fared worst of all, according to their tour manager, Anto. 'We were trying to get on a coach outside our hotel, and there were about fifteen local security men trying to help us. Bryan decided to run for it, but the security guys couldn't keep up with him, so the *fans* caught him instead! His CD player went, his CD collection, and when he got on to the bus he had no shoes! He was fairly scared! In some countries, if the girls are really mad about the band, their boyfriends get jealous, and one guy got to Bryan and punched him and pulled his hair. But it was his own fault – if he had done as he was told and not started running, he'd still have his shoes and an extra clump of hair.'

But all was not lost: the next time the band were in Asia, a fan sent back one of his shoes in a box!

Ha, ha . . . fooled again

Despite the hard work, the band always manage to have a load of laughs wherever they go, and the unwary band member who nods off can sometimes provide hours of amusement for the others!

The boys have found that it's particularly dangerous to fall asleep on a plane if Anto is in a mischievous mood . . . 'We were flying into Poland, and I was asleep on the plane,' says Mark. 'When I woke up, I was getting very, very suspicious looks from everybody – the air hostesses and other passengers. I thought it was because I had a dozy head on me, having just woken up. But as we were walking through the airport I noticed other people looking sideways at me. Eventually, we got to the hotel and there were a few fans waiting for autographs and they were all giggling. Obviously, the lads had been walking behind me, going "Shush!" When I got to my room, I went into the bathroom and dunked my face in some water. And when I looked in the mirror I saw that Anto had painted my face with a red marker! I had two round rosy cheeks and a red nose. I was very tired, so it was a while before I saw the funny side!'

No one was safe from the demon marker, as Nicky explains: 'On another flight, everyone was asleep except Bryan and me, and Bryan got a black permanent marker and wrote "FRED" across Mark's face, and he wrote "ED" on Kian's chin and then drew loads of lines on Shane's face. Then I was afraid I'd get blamed, so I got the marker and scribbled on my own face, and then went to sleep, just to be sure. It was great fun, because, when we landed in Heathrow, Shane woke up and looked at the rest of us and pretended there was nothing wrong, and then Mark woke up and saw us and smiled and said nothing. Bryan and I were in stitches laughing – particularly when Mark and Shane got to a mirror!'

All the travelling has ensured that there is a trail of Westlife lost property all around the globe, and sometimes this can be used to wind someone up. 'We were flying to Amsterdam, and Kian fell asleep, so Anto slipped off his new five-thousand-pound Rolex watch and put it on his own wrist,' says Shane. 'We got off the plane and were walking through the terminal when Kian started freaking out, shouting "Oh, God, me watch is gone!" He had only had it about a week at this stage! We hadn't seen Anto take it, so we were all asking him if he'd got it insured, and he's going, "No, no," and almost crying. Then Anto turns around and sticks out his arm and Kian went ballistic. He lost his head totally!'

However, the practical joke that Anto is most proud of

involved poor Bryan. 'It was in the early days of the band, and we were staying in a hotel in Sheffield. Bryan wanted to buy a pellet gun, which I thought was a really bad idea. But he went ahead and got it anyway.

'The next morning we were all leaving the hotel about eight a.m. to drive to London. Everyone's waiting in the lobby except Bryan. Then suddenly this woman comes running into the hotel going, "Call the police, call the police! There's a madman firing a gun outside!" I realised immediately that it was Bryan, and spent ages trying to persuade the receptionist not to call the police. I had just convinced her, when Bryan strolls downstairs looking innocent. He tried to deny he was the guilty party at first, but he finally confesses and apologises to the poor woman, who had just been minding her own business, walking her dog.'

That night, the band arrived in London and Anto decided to teach Bryan a lesson. 'I rang up a mate of mine, Liam, who was a policeman in London. As luck would have it, he was out on patrol, so I got him to drop into the hotel in full uniform. Bryan had gone to bed, so I ring his room and say, "Get downstairs now. There's a policeman here who wants to question you about the gun incident." So he came downstairs looking like a ghost.

'So my mate asked him if he owns a gun, and Bryan admitted that he had fired off a pellet gun. So then Liam tells him to pack a bag and accompany him to the station, and asks him if he has a solicitor. At this stage, Bryan is not a happy camper, and I'm standing there saying, "I can't help you with this one." Then Liam said, "I need you to come along peacefully, but first I want you to read this piece of paper so you know where you stand." He hands him his policeman's notebook, where there is just one word written on it — "GOTCHA"! Bryan reads it and just loses his head, and goes storming back up the stairs, shouting, "I can't believe you got me out of bed for that!" We all laughed for days over that one.'

Homeward bound . . .

Much as the band love visiting new places and meeting new fans — and they all love cities such as Sydney and Los Angeles — their favourite journey is the plane into Ireland.

'If we've been away for ages, maybe touring all over Asia or America, there's nothing like the excitement of coming home,' says Shane. 'Last summer when we were coming home from America after a seven-week tour, I was unbelievably wired! I laid out all my clothes and shower stuff the night before, so I could get to the airport as quick as possible! And we love seeing the Aer Lingus plane — we call it the Big Green Bird. And as soon as I saw the plane, I was jumping around, going, "Nicky look! It's the Big Green Bird!" And then we get aboard and there's these lovely women smiling and saying, "Howarya, lads? Would ye like a cuppa tea?" And were all shouting, "Yee-ha! We're going home!" '

Profile: Shane

FULL NAME:	**Shane Steven Filan**
DATE OF BIRTH:	**5 July 1979**
STAR SIGN:	**Cancer**
MUM AND DAD:	**Mae and Peter**
BROTHERS/SISTERS:	**Finbarr, Peter, Liam, Yvonne, Denise and Mairead**
HEIGHT:	**5ft 9in**
COLOUR OF EYES:	**Hazel/green**
ANY SCARS OR TATTOOS?	**Just a couple of small scars**

What do the rest of Westlife think of Shane?

Bryan: Shane is so talented. If I'm having problems getting a song right, I'll go to Shane for help. He can be really lively one minute and then he'll suddenly go really quiet. He loves getting out and meeting the fans.

Kian: Shane and I are very close. We're both very committed to making this band as successful as we can. We spend ages talking about songs, and about how the band is getting on. He's good fun to be with and, when we go home, we always go out together.

Nicky: Shane is sometimes very serious, and sometimes he's off-the-wall mad. He's great to talk to about anything, and he thinks about things very deeply. He's got very strongly held ideals.

Mark: He's very talented and great crack to be around — he's extremely funny and can have us in stitches in minutes. He's very generous and kind-hearted. Shane has a million-watt mega-smile that can light up the darkest room! He's always quietly bubbling over with ideas and plans for the future, both for himself and the band. And he's the boy who can't say no: when it comes to signing autographs for Westlife fans, Shane is always there to the end, making sure no one goes home empty-handed. And he loves animals, especially dogs and horses, almost as much as people, and he also has a passion for cars — fast cars, naturally. And girls — three things to remember: he's very romantic, he's a bit of a whiz in the kitchen, and he's very ticklish.

Shane in his own words

My earliest memory: I remember my first day at school. My mum brought me in, and I was bawling, crying. She had to lift me up for a big kiss — I was an awfully small child; no one thought I was going to grow! She left me in the class-room and, about an hour later, my older brother Finbarr came up to the window, looked in and pulled a huge face! I started to roar . . .

My first kiss: I was ten the first time, and I thought it was a bit weird. When I was twelve, I tried it again. It was a bit sloppy, and I didn't know what to do. I wasn't sure what she thought about me afterwards because she was more experienced than I was. But between thirteen and seventeen I put in a lot of practice! I had to have a new girlfriend every week!

My ideal girl: With the band, it's very difficult. I date whenever I can, but it's hard for me to trust girls now, and to find one who loves me for who I am, and who is happy chilling out on a couch watching videos, rather than going to parties every night. I love good-looking girls with long legs who wear short skirts and high heels. I love girls who look after themselves, but I don't like them plastered in make-up. I hate girls who talk too much, but I have to be able to have a laugh with them, and they have to like what I do for a living. I hate big-headed girls, even if they are beautiful.

[Erm a bit fussy, then Shane?] I *am* fussy, but girls are very important to me, so I have to get the right one!

My perfect day: I'd like to wake up somewhere in the countryside, and have a big breakfast out on a patio in front of a lake. Then I'd go for a walk with my beautiful wife and two kids — a girl and a boy. We'd stroll down to the lake that would have a few swans, and just relax. Then I'd go horse riding, have a big dinner with a few glasses of red wine, then go to bed and snuggle up. Someday, I'm going to sit at that lake and look back over a good and happy life.

Q&A
Who is your best friend in the band?
All four of them.
Are you a morning person or a night owl?
Night owl.

Do you read your horoscope?
Sometimes, but not much.

Do you believe in aliens? If so, what do you imagine they look like?
Yes. I'd say they're very weird-looking!

What was the first record you ever bought?
Billy Joel's 'Uptown Girl'.

How useful are you in the kitchen? What can you rustle up if you have to?
I'm very good in the kitchen – lasagne, spaghetti Bolognese, Irish fry and steak.

What part of your body would you change, if you could (keep it clean, lads)?
My feet!

Would you consider cosmetic surgery?
Never, unless I got badly burned in an accident.

Are you ticklish? If so, where (careful now)?
Yes. Everywhere!

What is the most expensive thing you've ever bought?
My Mitsubishi Pajero jeep.

What is the most useless thing you have ever bought?
A couple of books, as I never read!

What is the worst present you've ever received?
Can't remember.

Have you ever been in hospital?
A few times, but never overnight.

What is your favourite breakfast?
An Irish fry-up cooked by my mum or dad.

Hangover cures — what is the most effective?
A large glass of water.

If you went on a blind date, who would you most like to find sitting on the bar stool?
Faith Hill.

Have you ever written poetry?
Maybe some silly poems when I was young.

What is your favourite TV programme?
Friends and *The Simpsons*.

What is your favourite item of clothing?
My black leather Diesel trousers.

What is your most embarrassing item of clothing?
I have a few!

What scares the living daylights out of you?
Rats and big roller coasters.

What is the last thing you lost?
My CD collection on a plane to Hong Kong.

What is your favourite smoochy record?
R Kelly's 'I Believe I Can Fly'.

You've recorded with Mariah — who's next for a duet (or sextet, whatever)?
I don't know yet.

Who is your favourite musician/actor/actress?
Bryan Adams, Tom Cruise and Nicole Kidman.

What are the best/worst films you have ever seen?
Armageddon was the best, and *The Talented Mr Ripley* was the worst.

What is the best book you have ever read?
I don't read books. Sorry!

Are you superstitious?
Not really.

Did you enjoy school? What was your favourite subject?

Yes. I liked maths, accounting and English.

What false name have you used in the past when checking into a hotel?

Ha, ha, I can't tell you, 'cos it's a secret!

Do you have a lucky charm? If so, what is it?

No. But I'm Irish, which is lucky anyway.

Are you romantic?

Very much so.

Have you ever had your heart broken? If so, when, and by whom?

No, thankfully.

How old were you when you had your first kiss? Did you enjoy it?

Ten. Not at first!

Where is your favourite place in the world?

Sydney, Australia.

Do you sing in the shower?

Yes, all the time.

Do you lose your temper easily?

If I get aggravated.

Do you cry easily?

Yes, unfortunately. Especially when I leave my mum and dad at home when I go away with the band.

What is the worst job you ever had?

I haven't had many jobs – I worked in a hardware store, but that was fun.

What is your favourite sport to watch and/or play?

Basketball, soccer, tennis.

If you weren't in a band, what do you think you'd be up to?

I'd probably be in college, studying accountancy.

What do you imagine your life will be like in ten years' time?

I haven't a clue — hopefully, I'll be healthy, happy and very successful.

6 Fame and Family Life

While life is one huge whirlwind for the band, they know that the madness, the media and the mobs of fans are all part of their job. But behind Bryan, Mark, Kian, Shane and Nicky are their families, who have also seen their own lives change as well, and fame can look quite different from their point of view!

Mae Filan

'The speed at which everything happened took us all by surprise, as nobody could have guessed that the band would go so far so quickly,' says Mae. 'Even Louis has said to me a couple of times, "Where would we all be if you hadn't made that call?"'

But Mae always had huge faith in her youngest child: 'I always knew he'd do something in the music business. He always loved it.' And, although he's zooming here, there and everywhere, Shane always finds time to phone home: 'He's very good about phoning us, particularly if he's travelling a lot. If he's flying from Italy to America, for example, he'll call before he leaves Italy, and then rings once he lands in America, just to let me know that he's arrived safely.'

As the Filans' restaurant is right in the heart of the town, it has become the first Sligo stopping-off point for Westlife fans. 'The fans are great, and we get a lot of visitors, as we are so easy to find,' says Mae. 'They sometimes bring me lovely presents, such as little figurines or photographs of Shane which they have taken themselves. One girl was sitting in the restaurant and asked me, "Has Shane ever sat in this seat?" I said, "Of course, he's sat in every seat over the years" – and she fainted dead away on the spot!'

Marie Feehily

'It all seemed to happen overnight,' says Marie. 'In a way, the most exciting time was the first summer that the band were together, when they toured Ireland doing the Beat on the Street live shows, because it was all so new to us. We couldn't believe we were seeing our boys arriving on a stage as a professional band, with people cheering them. I remember going to see them play in Ballina in County Mayo, and Mark walked on to the stage in a denim suit and a new haircut, and I thought to myself, That's not the same lad I waved off from Sligo last week! After that, nothing was a shock!'

And even though the Feehilys live outside the town, it doesn't stop the fans from making the trip to see Mark's house – and some of them travel quite a distance! 'One night last winter, I left the house to put out some rubbish, and it was really pitch dark and creepy. Next thing, I heard some shouting, and I looked down the drive and there were two Australian fans waiting in the darkness. They were afraid to come up, because they had spotted our black Labrador, who probably looked even blacker and scarier in the winter night!'

Marie says all the family are 'delighted and proud' of Westlife's success: 'Even though he's always on the phone, I do miss Mark around the house. Growing up, he was always the life and soul of the place, running in and out doing things – except first thing in the morning, of course!'

Patricia Egan

'Even as a small child, Kian was determined to make it in the music business. He never had any doubt in his mind at all,' says Patricia. 'He was good at anything he tried in performance – music, acting. And he had a cute little face, which helped!'

Kian with little brother Colm

But Kian's not a superstar in his own home: 'Even though he's away a lot, we're still a very close family and we just have a normal life, which is what Kian really wants when he gets home from his travels. When he gets in after a trip, he just empties his suitcase on to the floor and heads off with his pals – or else brings his friends home with him. When Kian's around, I'm not just cooking for him, but for half of Sligo!'

And outside the Egan home it's all a bit different: 'As soon as we walk out the door, it seems like everyone knows us. Before the band, I could walk into town in fifteen minutes. Now it takes twice that, as people want to stop for a chat. But it's all goodwill, which is heart-warming.'

Mairead MacFadden

Unsurprisingly, the MacFadden home is noticeably quieter without Bryan. 'I miss him singing around the house, running up and down the stairs or standing with his bottom sticking out of the fridge!' says Mairead.

When Bryan first started travelling with the band, his mum was a bit worried about him, as he hadn't travelled much without his family before. 'I was packing his case before he went to England, and I was throwing in headache tablets, and chapsticks and tissues and vitamins, but he knows how to take care of himself now!' Still, she's happiest when she knows where her son is in the world – although sometimes, Bryan's not even sure himself.

Like the rest of the mums, Mairead deals with a lot of fan mail for her son. 'Most of the fans are lovely, and we try to give them something when they call, like a poster. But we've nothing left now!' And sometimes some of the letters can be a bit confusing: 'I opened one fan letter from a girl in Indonesia, and it sounded like she was close to dying. She talked about not having much time left, and that all she wanted was an autograph. I was in tears reading it. She had sent a stamped, addressed envelope, so I got the autograph and sent it back with a nice letter. Sometime later, the girl wrote back. She wasn't dying – she was moving house.'

Yvonne Byrne

Although all the Westlife boys made it into the newspaper headlines very quickly, Nicky beat the rest of them by a short blond head . . . 'While the auditions were still going on,' says Yvonne 'the family went to Lanzarote for a holiday. When we landed on the island, I picked up an Irish paper in the airport, and there on the front page was a headline, "THE POP STAR AND THE PRIME MINISTER'S DAUGHTER". I couldn't believe it!'

Yvonne also gets lots of fan mail for Nicky arriving at their Dublin home – she is amazed that some of the letters make it at all: 'We get mail from Asia and Australia which is just marked "Nicky, Westlife, Ireland" and it reaches us. Even Nicky's granny got a letter, addressed to "Nicky's Gran"!'

And all of Nicky's family are thrilled with his success: 'Even his granddad, who's seventy-three, is able to tell us what's Number One in the pop charts! And all the family drop in when Nicky's home. He just loves to unwind and lie on the couch and watch television, play lots of golf and foot-ball, and spend time with Georgina.'

A family surprise

Sometimes the families get the chance to turn the tables on their famous sons. One of the biggest shocks the boys ever got was when their five mums turned up as a surprise on a British TV show!

On Friday 31 March 2000, the band were being inter-viewed on *GMTV*, just before they left for America. Then the presenter, Lorraine Kelly, announced that, as it was almost Mother's Day, they were being treated to a live video link to their mums, who were in a Dublin studio. But, as the screen showed a studio with five empty chairs, Marie, Mae, Patricia, Yvonne and Mairead walked on the GMTV set! The boys were totally shocked – especially Bryan, as his mum had just got out of hospital a few days before. 'The lads nearly died when we walked out,' says Mairead. 'Everyone was very emotional – even the TV people were crying!'

But Mark nearly ruined the surprise when he decided to phone his mum just before they went on the show to make sure she had the telly on in Sligo! 'We were hiding in a room in the TV station, just after 8 a.m.,' says Marie, 'when one of the researchers ran in and said that Mark was on the phone to Sligo, looking for me!' Mark's quick-thinking dad told him that Marie was in the bath. 'I'm usually getting his brothers ready for school at that hour, so he couldn't figure out what I'd be doing in the bath. But he never guessed what was going on!'

The freedom of Sligo

It had been raining all day, but the clouds parted over Sligo just in time for Westlife's big moment.

On Saturday 1 July 2000, the five boys were given the Freedom of Sligo – even though two of them are Dubs!

For hours before the band arrived, hundreds of girls lined up along the barriers around Sligo City Hall, singing Westlife songs and clutching autograph books and 'WE LOVE WEST-LIFE' banners.

Finally, the band arrived, and walked along the barrier hugging fans and signing autographs, before being brought into the council chamber to receive their scroll and their key from the Lord Mayor, Rosaleen O'Grady. And the Lord Mayor was quick to remind Mark that she had first held him when he was just a few hours old, when she was in the same maternity ward as his mum!

It was a formal ceremony, but, as usual, the boys were able to raise a laugh. Mark and Kian and Shane thanked everyone in their speeches and talked about how proud they were to get such an honour – but it was the two Dubs who stole the show! Nicky got a huge cheer when he stood up and said his thank-you entirely in Irish, and then Bryan stood up and said, 'I just can't believe Nicky's just stolen my speech!'

He just never stops, does he?

7 It's Fun Being Famous

Spend, spend, spend . . .

If you're ever in America, and you know Westlife are in town, there's one place you will definitely find them . . . the shopping mall! These guys were born to shop till they drop. And guess who loves to shop the most . . .

'I'm the biggest impulse buyer in the world!' says Bryan. 'I love shopping in Los Angeles, because the clothes are so cool . . . I was in a leather shop there in the summer, and I couldn't decide between a red and a black jacket. So I bought them both, even though they were eight hundred pounds each or something crazy. I wore them once! I bought a little scooter for a thousand pounds, but then broke it. The most stupid thing I ever bought was this horrible shirt with pink panthers all over it! And when we opened the Harrods sale in July I bought forty-seven things, but only two were for myself: the rest were presents. I was going to buy myself a laptop computer, but I reckoned I'd only break it. Break it first, then lose it, probably!'

Being famous does mean that privacy becomes a bit of a problem, unless you're Mark 'Invisible Man' Feehily. 'In Ireland it can be difficult, but anywhere else it's possible to walk around unnoticed. I just stick on a baseball cap and dress casually. I don't think I have a noticeable face, though. But if you dress up in sunglasses and a flashy suit like some stars do, and walk around with a security guard, then people aren't stupid. You're gonna get followed.'

Girls, girls, girls . . .

Surely being followed by lots of gorgeous lassies isn't so terrible? But, oddly enough, the boys all confess that being in a big pop band actually makes it harder for them to meet the girl of their dreams.

Kian learned the hard way about kiss-and-tell girls, when, in May 1999, one of the newspapers ran a story spilling all the details about a naughty night he had spent with an English barmaid, eighteen-year-old Emma Robertson. 'The story was front-page news in Ireland, where we had just gone to Number One with "Swear It Again". I cried my eyes out when I saw it, but it taught me a lesson,' says Kian.

'Now I can spot very quickly if a girl is interested in me, or just in what I do for a living. And I might meet a beautiful girl one night, and think, Hey, I wouldn't mind spending a little time getting to know her. But then the next day I'm climbing on a plane to go halfway round the world. It can be tough.'

Shane agrees with Kian. 'I'd love to meet Miss Right and fall madly in love. Some days I wake up and think, Maybe today I'm going to meet the girl of my dreams, because you never know when she could be around the next corner. I'm a bit of a romantic like that! But even if I met someone really special tomorrow I don't know if I could make a relationship work . . . we move around so much. But someday . . .'

Bryan's love life often makes it into the newspapers, but he insists that most of the stories are wrong. 'It makes me laugh when I see stories about me dating Miss World, or that I was spotted on a date with Janey from Hepburn, when I had actually been out with herself and her boyfriend that night! The trouble is that a lot of our fans don't realise that these stories are bull! But I absolutely love going out and meeting girls in different cities. I'm a hopeless romantic at heart.'

Mark, too, finds meeting girls difficult: 'I'm bad at going up to girls and starting a conversation. I don't have much confidence, and I won't move unless they show some interest first! The sort of girls I like are outgoing and not afraid to start chatting. But I have to feel that they are interested in me, rather than the fact that I'm in a band.'

It's different for Nicky, as he has Georgina, his girlfriend of five years. 'It's hard for both of us to be separated from each other so much, but we're still as close as ever. The difference is that she got to know me before I was a footballer or a singer, and she knows the real me. I can always ring her up at any time if there's something worrying me, and she always manages to calm me down!'

The Sound of Music – How do you greet a pop star like Mariah?

Sometimes, Westlife get to meet celebrities who are actually more famous than they are. In the past few crazy years, they've shaken hands with all sorts of megastars. At the preshow Grammy Awards party in Los Angeles, they walked into the hotel alongside artists such as Britney Spears, Stevie Wonder and Cameron Diaz. They sang 'Swear It Again' with Mohammed al-Fayed on Shane's 21st birthday in July 2000 when they opened the Harrods sale. In May, when they put on a special performance for one of the richest men in the world, the Sultan of Brunei, they had a ball. After the show, the Sultan's son drove the lads around the palace grounds in his Porsche. Car-mad Kian was green with envy . . .

Even meeting Queen Elizabeth didn't rattle the Westlife boys. The lads were introduced to her in December 1999 after they played at the Royal Variety Performance in London. And Nicky had a bad moment – when she stopped and spoke to him, he couldn't hear what she had said. 'I just thought, Oh my God! and tried to think up something that would do as an answer to whatever she'd said to me. So I just replied, "It was great to be here and we really enjoyed ourselves." Afterwards, Shane told me that she'd said, "Thank you for taking the time out to come here." So that worked out well!'

Then Bryan decided to have a chat – strictly against orders! 'As we were lining up to meet her, this man with a stick and a hat came up and told us we had to speak when we were spoken to, and told us how to address her, and which way to stand. I thought she might be bored with all that, so, as she was walking away from us, I said, "By the way, ma'am, your dress is lovely," and she said, "Why, thank you." She didn't seem to mind!'

But the one time that the five boys found themselves star-struck was when they met Mariah Carey – especially her biggest fan, Mark Feehily. 'I've always been a fan of Mariah's.

When I was younger, I'd be in my room, listening to her CDs and singing into a hairbrush in front of the mirror, pretending I was singing with her!'

Then, to his joy, he came face to face with the American superstar at the launch of the MTV Europe Award nominations in 1999, when he was invited to meet her. 'I was determined not to look like an eejit, so I grabbed a CD for her to autograph and rehearsed what I was going to say as I walked to where she was sitting. I was just going to keep calm, shake her hand and say, 'Pleased to meet you, Mariah. I'm a big fan. Would you mind signing this for me?'

'But I went totally blank as soon as I saw her. I just stood there staring at her, and just muttered, "Hi, I'm Mark," and just held out the CD without saying a word!'

But he had a chance to redeem himself when the band met Mariah again in Los Angeles. 'I was a bit more relaxed this time, and actually managed to talk, until she suggested doing a song together. My jaw just hit the floor!' says Mark.

And in May 2000 Mark's lifelong dream came true when Westlife travelled to the island of Capri off the Italian coast, to record their duet, 'Against All Odds'.

'When we arrived at Naples airport, we were met by one of Mariah's guys. We were used to travelling in a van, but this guy leads us to four stretch limos for the six of us, the band and Anto!' says Mark. 'Then he brought us to the biggest and most beautiful yacht I've ever seen – it was bigger than some hotels we've stayed in! We had to take off our shoes when we went aboard!'

Later that evening, the band were having supper in the

hotel, when Mariah suddenly appeared. 'At first, none of us would say a word to her,' says Mark, 'but she just sat down and started chatting to us. She was really down to earth, and soon we were teaching her some Irish slang, like "What's the story?" and "How's the *craic*?" '

Even being in the same studio as Mariah felt unreal to the boys: 'I stuck on the headphones, and I could see her watching me through the glass, and I thought to myself, Here goes – if I mess this up, I'll kick myself for ever! And when we made the video together she looked so beautiful that I had to keep pinching myself to see whether it was all a dream.'

But it wasn't just Mark who was feeling a bit nervous: 'She kept asking us our opinions during the recording session,' says Kian. 'We were just going, "Whatever you want is fine," and she was saying, "No, no! Tell me what you guys want!" It was incredible. I'll remember that day when I'm seventy.'

Profile: Bryan

FULL NAME:	**Bryan Nicholas MacFadden**
DATE OF BIRTH:	**12 April 1980**
STAR SIGN:	**Aries**
MUM AND DAD:	**Mairead and Brendan**
BROTHERS/SISTERS:	**Just the one, my sister Susan**
HEIGHT:	**6 ft**
COLOUR OF EYES:	**Blue**
ANY SCARS OR TATTOOS:	**None, really**

What do the rest of Westlife think of Bryan?

Shane: It's hard to describe him! He's full of laughs, full of jokes. You never know what he's going to say or do next! He's a very nice guy – he's not afraid to talk about serious things; he'll sit down and discuss girls or his family or the band. He's all heart. Bryan thinks he's a bit cool, but he's really a softie!

Mark: Bryan is an out-and-out nutter, although he has calmed down a bit recently. You just don't know what he's going to do next – one minute, he's moaning about being too tired to go out, then, five minutes later, he's trying to round up a crowd to go clubbing! He's utterly unpredictable.

Kian: Bryan is a lunatic! He's got a great view of life: he just lives for today, and lets tomorrow look after itself. He's serious about his work, but he knows when to relax, and will start telling the rest of us to chill out, if we're getting a bit intense.

Nicky: Bryan's a fellow Dub, so we gelled from the start. He's always on the go, a bubbly personality. He's always trying to make you laugh, and he lives life a day at a time. He'll spend hundreds of pounds on something at the drop of a hat, and then just laugh and say, 'We might all be dead tomorrow.' I respect him for that, because I worry about everything. Bryan never gets lost, because he can always be heard singing at the top of his voice, or talking nonstop. He doesn't even stop moving in his sleep, as he sometimes gets up and goes for a stroll while still in the Land of Nod!

He's famous for losing things, and Bryan's possessions are scattered all over five continents, but he rarely misses any of the stuff, as this shopaholic just nips out to the nearest store and buys more! Our producer Pete Waterman describes Bryan as 'one of the funniest people I've ever met' and admitted he usually has to leave the room when Bryan starts some of his wicked impressions!

Bryan in his own words

My favourite place: My favourite place in Ireland is Donegal, but I've seen some fantastic places outside Ireland. I love Thailand, Los Angeles, New York, Florida. But the trouble is that we don't appreciate travelling that much as it's just part of our job. It's like someone who passes a lovely waterfall on his or her way to work and doesn't notice its beauty after a while. I'd love to travel the world with some friends and see it properly. No rucksack, though! I never want to carry a bag ever again! I'll just buy new clothes everywhere I go!

My earliest memory: I remember being in Donegal at Christmas when I was three. It was the first time I woke up in someone else's house on Christmas Day, and I was afraid that Santa wouldn't find me. He did of course!

My first kiss: I didn't have my first proper kiss until I was sixteen. She was at Billie Barry's [stage school] and we went on a date to the cinema. I was really nervous, and didn't know when to make a move. Luckily, she was more experienced than me, and when we finally kissed it was a bit weird because I was so scared! But I took to kissing in a big way after that!

My ideal girl: She would have to like the same things that I do – someone who likes a laugh. I love a girl who isn't obsessed by the way she looks. My ideal girl can wake up in the morning with no make-up on, and her hair tied back, and she still looks beautiful. I know she's out there – I just have to find her . . .

Q&A
Who is your best friend in the band?
Me!
Are you a morning person or a night owl?
A morning person.
Do you read your horoscope?
Sometimes.
Do you believe in aliens? If so, what do you imagine they look like?
Yes – I suspect they look like our tour manager, Anto Byrne!
What was the first record you ever bought?
Kylie Minogue's 'I Should Be So Lucky'.

How useful are you in the kitchen? What can you rustle up if you have to?

I'm hopeless.

What part of your body would you change, if you could (keep it clean, lads)?

I'd change all of it, apart from my heart and mind.

Would you consider cosmetic surgery?

No!

Are you ticklish? If so, where (careful now)?

Yes, but I'm not telling you where!

What is the most expensive thing you've ever bought?

A £5,000 watch.

What is the most useless thing you've ever bought?

A shirt with pink panthers all over it!

What is the worst present you've ever received?

A turnip from a fan!

Have you ever been in hospital?

Yes.

What is your favourite breakfast?

A big fry-up.

Hangover cures — what is the most effective?

More drink!

If you went on a blind date, who would you most like to find sitting on the bar stool?

Lulu or my nanny.

Have you ever written poetry?

Yes.

What is your favourite TV programme?

Friends.

What is your favourite item of clothing?
I love hooded jumpers.

What is your most embarrassing item of clothing?
A shredded jacket.

What scares the living daylights out of you?
Dentists. Hate 'em.

What is the last thing you lost?
A watch I got from someone special.

What is your favourite smoochy record?
'If Tomorrow Never Comes'.

You've recorded with Mariah — who's next for a duet (or sextet, whatever)?
Stevie Wonder.

Who is your favourite musician?
Bryan Adams.

What are the best/worst films you ever saw?
The best was *The Green Mile*, the worst *Patch Adams*.

What is the best book you have ever read?
Powder by Kevin Sampson.

Are you superstitious?
Yes.

Did you enjoy school? What was your favourite subject?
No. But I enjoyed English.

What false name have you used in the past when checking into a hotel?
Homer Simpson!

Do you have a lucky charm? If so, what is it?
A little Chinese pouch, but I'm not supposed to know what's inside it.

Are you romantic?

Yes, very romantic.

Have you ever had your heart broken? If so, when, and by whom?

Yes.

How old were you when you had your first kiss? Did you enjoy it?

I was sixteen — and, no, I didn't enjoy it at all!

Where is your favourite place in the world?

Donegal, Ireland.

Do you sing in the shower?

Yes, very loudly!

Do you lose your temper easily?

No, I'm pretty relaxed most of the time.

Do you cry easily?

Yes.

Westlife: In Real Life

What is the worst job you ever had?
Shovelling burgers in McDonald's.
What is you favourite sport to watch and/or play?
Soccer and golf.
If you weren't in a band, what do you think you'd be up to?
I'd be in a different band!
What do you imagine your life will be like in ten years' time?
I'll be married, I'll have two kids — a boy and a girl — and I'll be living in a big house somewhere in Ireland with my beautiful wife.

8 A Weekend with Westlife – Party in the Park

Friday 7 July 2000

Aer Lingus flight E1858 lands in London City Airport right on schedule. On board are the three Sligo lads, Mark, Shane and Kian, along with their reassuringly solid security man, Paul Higgins, and their tour manager, Anto Byrne. Bryan and Nicky are due to follow the tomorrow morning.

The band's flight was booked only the night before, but Westlife fans could teach the police a thing or two when it comes to sniffing out information, and there are four girls waiting for the lads as they come into the arrivals hall.

As the two cars drive through London, Shane notices that the girls from the airport are in a taxi behind. The driver spots them, too, and turns left suddenly, darting down a side street, leaving the taxi cab stranded. Shane waves out of the window: 'Bye-bye, girls.'

But the last laugh is on Shane – when his car pulls up outside the hotel, the girls are there ahead of him! The band are staying in the very posh Mandarin Oriental hotel in Knightsbridge – the sort of place where there's always a bloke in a red coat with shiny gold buttons standing at the door.

By the time the lads check into the hotel, it's 9 p.m., and Kian and Shane decide to have an early night – but Mark is up for checking out the London nightlife. He's invited a mate of his from Sligo to London for the weekend, and the pair of them are anxious to go clubbing: 'It's great to have someone from home here for the weekend. It's important to make an effort to see my mates as often as I can – it keeps me grounded, so there's no danger of me turning into an obnoxious brat!' he laughs.

Mark and his pal and Paul Higgins head for Sugar Reef in Soho, and then on to HOME dance club in Leicester Square. It's after midnight, and a long queue snakes along the street from the club's door – but, as luck would have it, Paul knows one of the doormen from Dublin. In an instant, everyone is whisked inside the velvet rope, with the invisible VIP stamp on the back of their hands. 'These velvet ropes are funny things,' muses Mark as he heads for the bar. 'They're in every nightclub, blocking off the VIP bar, or whatever. And when you're the far side of the rope you really want to be inside it, and yet a lot of VIP areas feel like zoos. Everyone outside the rope is staring in at you, and everyone inside the rope is staring at each other! It's weird . . .'

Eventually, HOME closes, and Mark stands on the street, munching on a hot dog and chatting to some girls he's met in the club. Paul taps him on the shoulder. 'C'mon Mark. It's four in the morning, and you're up in four hours.' Mark puts on a brave face, and heads off in search of a taxi. When it comes to finding a cab in central London on a Saturday night, all men – and pop stars – are equal . . .

Saturday 8 July 2000

It's 9 a.m., and the boys are up and moving. They drag their big, battered, black suitcases down to the hotel lobby and out into the waiting cars. Tonight they're staying in the Metropolitan Hotel, which is close to Hyde Park: 'It's very easy to forget where you are, if you wake up in the middle of the night in a hotel,' says Shane. 'I once woke up in a hotel in Australia, and I didn't have a clue where I was. I thought I was heading for the bathroom, but then I banged into the window. I couldn't find the lights, or the phone, and I couldn't remember what country I was in.'

So he panicked, right? 'Nah – I just went to sleep and hoped I'd know where I was in the morning.' These boys are made from stern stuff, and no mistake.

By 10 a.m., the band have arrived at a rehearsal studio, the Worxx, for two photo shoots and interviews for *Top of the Pops* and *TV Hits* magazines. The studio is a hive of activity, with clothes and hair stylists, make-up artists and a photographer all milling about, waiting to pounce on the boys.

Getting the five boys ready for the photo shoot takes surprisingly long – they don't actually step in front of a camera until almost 1 p.m. The hair stylist, Ben, gets busy on Mark's hair with sharp scissors, and gives him a no-messing, tight cut. Then Mark moves on to the make-up girl, and then on to wardrobe, like a tin of peas on a conveyor belt.

But the studio isn't quiet – far from it. Shane and Bryan and Mark have been singing all morning – Bryan in particular never stops singing, never stops moving. He whizzes around the studio and down the corridors on a small, silver scooter which he bought when the band opened the Harrods sale earlier that week. He tries on his stage clothes for the next day, and takes a fancy to the lovely grey three-quarter-length Alexander MacQueen coat that the stylists Dave and Nikki have found for him. 'I like this,' he says, admiring it in the mirror. Five minutes later it is thrown over the back of a chair, forgotten.

Finally, the photographer's ready. Martin Gardener has snapped the lads several times before. 'The first time I took pictures of Westlife was when they were in Stockholm recording their first album. Nobody knew who they were yet, but a bunch of girls were still camped outside their hotel,' says Martin. 'Every time one of the boys looked out the window, the girls lifted their shirts – even though it was the middle of winter and the snow was pelting down!'

There isn't any snow falling on the Worxx, but there are fans outside – the same four girls are spending their day keeping vigil on the studio. Blonde Natalie, Little Natalie, Sarah and Mel are dedicated Westlife fans, and follow the band any time they're in England, tracking their movements through a complicated network of email, text messages and parental help – one of the girls' parents works for an airline. 'We went to New York to see them once. We took a week off school and college, and ended up staying in the same hotel as the band,' they say.

The boys eventually take a break for lunch – which consists of disgusting chicken burgers and soggy chips – 'I'm

Louis Walsh and Sonny from RCA Records singing in the rain

gonna regret this for the rest of the day,' sighs Kian as he nibbles unenthusiastically on a half-cold burger.

Then it's back to the photo session. The boys run about, pulling on various trousers and tops; Kian puts on a garish tight jungle-print top.

'This is cool for the cover shot, isn't it?' he asks.

'If the cover was in black and white, maybe,' mutters one of his pals uncharitably.

'Maybe a black top would be better, Kian,' suggests Dave the stylist.

In the meantime, Anto sits at the table, hunched over a borrowed PC – 'Nicky broke my other one,' he explains – and keeping an eye on proceedings. 'Anyone not working?'

he calls out as some of the boys potter by. 'If so, start signing these photographs,' he says, pushing a stack of glossy pics across the table. No rest for the talented . . .

Then there is a new arrival: Andrew Berkowitz from Arista, who looks after the band's TV and radio promotions in America, bursts through the door, fresh – or boggle-eyed – off a flight from Los Angeles. After hugs all around, Andrew pulls out a stack of photographs of the boys, taken during their trip around the US in June.

The second photo shoot begins, and the journalists from the two magazines interview each of the guys in turn. Anto looks at his watch: 4 p.m. Time to move on.

The lads pile into two cars and head back into the Pineapple Studios in Covent Garden for dance and singing rehearsals for tomorrow's show. Nicky promptly falls asleep in the front seat of the car until he's nudged awake outside Pineapple. He opens his eyes – only to find the car surrounded by about fifty girls. 'Oh my God – where are we?' he mutters, confused.

Helped by Paul, their very own human brick wall, the lads squeeze through the camera-waving scrum into the studio. They troop into Studio 9, where their choreographer, Paul Domain, waits. Bryan sits down at a piano and starts playing: 'I taught myself how to play, but I'd love to learn properly. No time, though,' he says.

Anto points to a round hole in the middle of the studio wall. 'Mark put his foot through the wall by accident the last time we were here. I hid the hole by taping a Pineapple notice over it, but they've obviously found it since.'

The boys sweat through a quick dance rehearsal with Paul, and then the gospel choir that will sing on stage with the band in the Park tomorrow turn up. Paul instructs them all where to stand, and they run through a couple of rehearsals – the sound of all the voices harmonising fills the little dance studio. 'That sounds good,' says Shane, smiling.

By 7 p.m., they're finished. They leave and spend ten minutes signing autographs for a big crowd of fans gathered in the rain outside the studio. Then it's back to the hotel. Sunday will be a big day, playing in front of 100,000 people, so none of the band are out on the town tonight – though they may have one quick drink in the hotel's super-cool Met Bar. Just the one . . .

It's early. Very early. But Bryan is indignant. He's just heard that Mark was asked to give up his seat in the Met Bar last night to make room for another star who was playing at the Party in the Park (OK, it was Christina Aguilera). 'These two big guys asked me to move, and I did, because I thought there was something wrong,' explains Mark, 'but then, when Christina sat down, I realised they were her security, and they just wanted to make sure that no one was sharing her seat!' Bryan is not amused, 'If I'd been there, I'd have shown them what's what,' he mutters darkly.

Sunday 9 July 2000

It's 8 a.m., and the band are up, dressed, with make-up firmly in place. It's a grey, chilly morning, and the rain is falling steadily on Hyde Park, but already the fans are streaming out of the tube stations, heading for the concert site. The band drive by, around to the backstage gate. 'Passes, please,' demands the guard. This is the first of countless times that the band will have to show their passes – silver and green plastic bracelets marked 'Artists', which give them access to everywhere.

And figuring out the pass system at the Party in the Park could be a good way for rocket scientists to exercise their grey matter when they want a challenge. There are green bracelets, silver bracelets, silver-and-green bracelets. There are stick-on passes. Artists Only. Crew Only. Artists' Crew Only. VIP Only. Guest Only. Press Only. There are passes for the record company hospitality tents. 'Sorry, miss. You can get on stage with that pass, but you can't get backstage.'

Huh?

Ben and Nikki, the hair and clothes stylists, have the wrong passes. Ten minutes and two arguments later, everyone is in. Backstage is a maze of white Portakabins, sitting on what is going to be a very muddy patch of grass.

Ben fiddles with the Westlife boys' damp locks. 'This weather will play hell with your hair,' he sighs, before they're led to a small stage for a live spot on the morning TV show, *T4*. It's 9 a.m., and the band are tired and wet as the rain spills down. Around them, insanely bubbly presenters chatter loudly into TV cameras as the band yawn on the little stage. But, as soon as the backing track to 'If I Let You Go' blares out, Kian, Nicky, Bryan, Shane and Mark swing into action, looking as if they'd had a full twelve hours' sleep, followed by a big Irish fry.

The insane presenters all cheer wildly, and the band are off again. A suite in the Hilton Hotel has been booked for a photo shoot for *Smash Hits*. But, before anyone points a camera in their direction, Bryan, Nicky and Kian head for breakfast. Kian piles his plate with food, then asks the waiter, 'Any chance of a few baked beans?' Over breakfast, they discuss a story that's appeared in one of the papers this morning, which claims that Britney Spears is engaged to Justin from 'N Sync. 'Just because they're engaged doesn't mean they're getting married . . .' says Nicky wisely.

Know much about engagements, then, Nicky? He throws his eyes up to heaven and laughs. 'No! I don't know a thing! I won't be thinking like that for a few years yet!'

The *Smash Hits* photo shoot drags on. Bryan gets to sit in a yellow sack, while the photographer's assistants throw fan mail on top of him. Kian dozes in a chair, while Ben sorts out his hair. Shane talks into another tape recorder: 'My taste in clothes has improved. For a while, the fashion police were after me . . .' he explains. Bryan bops around, playing with a baby turtle which one of the *Smash Hits* journalists has brought. He lifts it up to his mouth: 'Hmm, crunchy!'

Meanwhile, Mark is trying to figure out how to pose with an ice cube, and Shane swings his photo prop, an old-fashioned suitcase. He snaps it open. 'Anyone wanna buy a watch?' He grins. Nicky curls up on the couch in the suite and rubs his elbow, which carries a long scar and an unnatural bump. 'It's an old football injury. There's a pin in my elbow which you can feel through the skin. It gets sore sometimes, and I love to rest it on something soft.'

Mmmm.

During the photo shoot, Paul is stretched out on the

floor, catching up on some sleep, while Anto lies beside the window, under his jacket. But he isn't asleep. He's on the phone, trying to organise hotel rooms in Dublin for the Sligo boys for the next two days. 'How about the Morrison? The Morgan? The Stakis? Come on, lads, make a decision,' he groans from under his jacket.

At 1 p.m., the band head back to the Metropolitan. A quick lunch, and then upstairs to do a spot for *SMTV*. The programme is due to celebrate its 100th show later that month, and the band film a spot in which they are decorating a chocolate birthday cake with handfuls of Smarties and and icing. Kian puts on a chef's hat and Nicky an apron — but no one mistakes them for Jamie Oliver . . .

In the middle of the chaos, Louis Walsh appears and greets the band: 'Nicky, your hair looks dreadful.'

It's now 3.30 p.m., and the band all climb into the cars for the five-minute drive to the Park.

By now, the rain is cascading down. The backstage area is a sea of mud, and the audience is a carpet of multicoloured umbrellas. It's a sad contrast to last year, when everyone sat around in blazing sunshine.

Most of the bands stay inside their Portakabins — although Kian slips out to the toilets to have a quick shave before going on stage, and he comes back wide-eyed. 'I was in the toilet having a shave, when one of the Backstreet Boys came in — and he had a security guard with him who stood back to back with him while he peed!'

By the time the boys are ready to go onstage, the rain is hammering down on the muddy grass — which presents a problem, as they are all wearing sharp white trousers! It's no time to be cool, so, with trousers rolled up to their knees and huddled under some borrowed umbrellas, they scuttle on stage. 'OK guys. Let's, erm, ballad this town!' shouts Shane.

Despite the sheets of rain, the boys get the crowd going. Their manager Louis slips on a plastic bin-liner style of rain mac and stands in the crowd watching them. Afterwards, Kian is happy: 'The rain was a shame, but the buzz on stage was brilliant, and all the umbrellas were bopping along to the music. It was our first big gig since our fifth Number One, so it was a bit of a celebration. When we walk on stage, it's like electricity running from your toes to the longest hairs on your head. Being on stage is the best part of being in the band, just to hear the crowd screaming and seeing banners with "Kian" written on them. I just think, That's me! It's a dreamlike feeling . . .'

Once off stage, Westlife — or Wetlife as they are now — hang around for a while, saying hello to friends and fans. Then it's into the cars, back to the hotel, pack, and drive to the airport for a flight home. As the band trail through Dublin airport at 10.30 p.m., Nicky remarks, 'That wasn't too hard a day, thank God.'

9 Another Weekend with Westlife – Recording in Sweden

Saturday 15 July 2000

It's pure bedlam in Dublin airport. Mid-afternoon in the height of the holiday season, the airport is a heaving mass of endless queues, excited children and mountains of luggage taking up every inch of remaining floor space. But where are Westlife? How on earth can anyone find five lads in this chaos?

In the end, it's easy. Just follow the camera flashes and the girls' voices: 'Kian! Sign this! Nicky, can I have a picture?' The boys are grouped at the British Midland check-in desk, on their way to Stockholm in Sweden to begin work on their second album. Shane looks a little pale – he is recovering from a bad dose of flu, which has forced the band to postpone their Swedish trip by four days.

On the first flight – to London Heathrow – Nicky recognises one of the air hostesses. 'D'you remember us?' he asks her. 'Oh, yes,' she says, 'but you've all grown up a bit since then, haven't you?'

And Nicky grins, while Anto explains, 'In the early days of the band, the record company used to fly the boys over and back to London in business class on British Midland. They were much rowdier back then, and they used to play this tipping game where they'd tip each other. Then the tip would turn into a shove, then the shove into a punch, and the punch into a full-on digging match! I couldn't believe their behaviour in first class, and neither could the air hostesses! So, Ronan was on a flight one day, and an air hostess had a quick word — and suddenly the band were flying in economy until they learned some manners!'

But, although the band are now all seasoned travellers, even Westlife have trouble with the sprawling maze of Heathrow Airport. Getting from Terminal 1 to Terminal 3 proves a little tricky, and Anto, with a face like a cross cherub, leads the boys up one escalator and straight down another.

'Jaysus, Anto, d'you know where you're going?' grumbles Kian.

'I haven't lost youse yet,' Anto replies, though he looks as if the idea appeals to him.

Waiting to board the plane to Stockholm, the five boys glue themselves to their phones. When not on stage or sleeping, at least one of Westlife will be yakking down the line to friends or family. 'It drives us all mad when we go to a place where our mobiles don't work, like in some parts of the States,' says Mark. 'You should see our hotel room bills then . . .'

Nicky settles himself into the plane seat, and hunts for the book he has just bought at the airport shop, *Powder* by Kevin Sampson, which is about the ups and downs of being in a band. 'Aw, no! I've left it on the shop counter,' he moans.

Losing things is a daily hazard for this bunch — with Bryan being the worst offender: in summer 2000 he lost his mobile phone in Thailand and it took him two long months to replace it. Then he lost his new one two weeks later.

'Bryan would lose his head if it wasn't tied to his shoulders,' says Mark. 'Sometimes if he's asleep on a flight, we'll hide his passport, and it's so funny to watch him running around in a panic, and he knows he'll be killed if he loses it. So he'll say, "Lads, I've left my Walkman on the plane," and he'll go running off. He wouldn't have a clue!' Hmm, lucky for the lads that Bryan's got a great sense of humour . . .

During the two-and-a-half-hour flight to Stockholm, Kian reads his book, *Tuesdays With Morrie* by Mitch Albom. 'It's brilliant,' he enthuses. 'It's all about how we should all just live for the day.' Anto looks worried . . .

Once the flight is airborne, the ever-hungry Nicky asks the Swedish air hostess, 'What kind of food is on this plane?' She looks puzzled, 'What kind of fuel?' she asks. Bryan listens to music on his DVD player, which is a mini video player and CD player rolled into one, while Shane sketches in his black Filofax. 'I'm building a new house in Sligo for my family,' he announces. 'I love sketching details of the rooms — it's going to be an old-style redbrick house, with nine bedrooms, a snooker room and bar, tennis courts, a basketball court, loads of garages, and land for the horses. A dream house for a big family.'

On landing, the boys are keen to go straight to the studios and hear their new songs, but it's too late. The rain is pouring down in dark sheets as the band leave the airport at about 9.30 p.m. They are greeted by a group of fans and press photographers. 'The fans here almost think of us as locals, as we recorded our first album here and spent quite a lot of time in Stockholm,' explains Kian.

During the drive to the hotel, Nicky ponders over the difference a year can make. 'It's so weird to be back here now. The last time we were here, no one knew us, and we were just starting out. It was the middle of winter and freezing cold, and I ended up getting pneumonia and flying home early. It's hard to believe that so much has happened since then.'

Despite the rain and the lateness of the hour, a crowd of blonde-haired girls are waiting for the band — one girl almost collapses in hysterics at the sight of the boys piling out of the van. Shane goes and gives her a hug, which reduces the lassie to a gibbering wreck. 'She's one of our regular fans,' he explains.

There are more fans than usual inside and outside the hotel — some girls book into the hotel for better access to the band — as the Backstreet Boys are also in residence. The lads all check in, and Kian and Bryan head straight for the hotel's small casino. 'I like gambling,' says Bryan, with a grin. 'But I'm more careful these days. When we were just starting out, I went into a casino in Amsterdam with fifty pounds. I won three thousand five hundred on blackjack by 3 a.m., and walked out of the place an hour later with empty pockets. I was well sick. Learned my lesson well, I can tell you.'

The next morning, the band set off for Cheiron Studios. The van crackles with nervous energy. They are dying to hear the new songs, but they're all tense too. As Westlife's first album exceeded everyone's hopes by selling over five million copies, the band have a lot to live up to now, and this is where it all begins. The van stops at a petrol station, and Bryan runs into the shop. He climbs back into the van clutching a hot dog. It smells like old socks. 'Uuurgh – open a window quickly,' yells Nicky, as everyone's eyes begin to water. 'There's no way I'm standing in a small, airless studio with you this afternoon,' Kian warns. Bryan tucks in, unruffled: 'It's a grand breakfast . . .'

The van pulls up at Cheiron. There are more fans outside. They sign autographs and then clatter anxiously down the wooden staircase to the studio, where the producers and writers are waiting. One of the writers smiles: 'We've some great songs for you. Particularly this first one.' He hits a switch, and 'I Lay My Love On You' thunders through the speakers. The five boys look at each other with ear-to-ear grins. Shane begins to sing along, eyes on the lyric sheet. It's a great pop song. Everything is going to be all right. They hug each other with excitement and relief. 'Cheiron is a fantastic studio,' says Shane. 'As soon as we heard "I Lay My Love On You", we loved it.'

And Cheiron is a shrine to successful pop acts: the walls of the narrow corridors are festooned with gold and platinum discs from bands who have been touched by the magic of the studio's founders Tom Talomaa and the late Dennis Pop, and more recently by the top producer/songwriter, Max Martin.

In Max's office, a forest of music awards stand jumbled on a cabinet, each bearing a plaque of unbelievable statistics: ten million sales of Britney Spears's album in the US; eleven million sales of the Backstreet Boys' *Millennium* album in the US. 'Maybe we'll be there next year,' says Nicky hopefully.

The awards remind Nicky of a hairy moment at the Record of the Year Awards in London last December. 'It was an amazing night,' he says. ' "Flying Without Wings" was neck and neck with Ronan's song, "When You Say Nothing At All", until the end, when we beat him by over nine thousand votes. It was like the Eurovision! When we were presented with our award, I ran down into the crowd to hug Wayne Hector, one of the writers of the song. I threw my arms around him, but I forgot I still had the award in my hand, and it hit something, and cracked right down the middle! In all the photos, I'm actually holding the award together!'

There's a lot of hanging about to be done in a recording studio. Each band member is taken in, one by one, to record vocals, so the rest have to amuse themselves in the meantime. Nicky drinks endless cups of tea — each heaped with three spoons of sugar! — and he takes on Kian at a Playstation game of basketball. Each match is fierce and competitive. Kian gets on a winning streak: 'Ah-*ha*! I'm the champion of the universe!' he crows, punching the air. Nicky is not amused — he hates losing. 'Another game, Kian? I'll stomp you this time for sure.'

And he does. He whoops and jumps on top of Kian: 'Who's champion now?' Then they settle in for a rematch . . .

In the meantime, Anto has been to the shops, and is busy in the small kitchen, preparing lunch of steak and pasta in sauce. 'You end up being so many things as tour manager —

a human alarm clock, a travel operator, a luggage finder, a big brother, and sometimes a cook. I hate to see the lads eating junk food all the time,' he explains.

As soon as the smell wafts through the studio, the boys pile into the kitchen and hoover up the food. But Shane pulls a face: 'Anto, this meat is very chewy,' he complains. Anto says nothing, but plots his revenge . . .

The Westlife boys love their food — although it is to be nearly Kian's undoing on their second night in Sweden.

They get back from the studio about 10.30 p.m., tired and ravenous, only to find that the hotel's kitchen has just closed. Kian, Bryan, Nicky and Anto debate what to do. Nicky and Anto find out that the only restaurant open on a Sunday night in Stockholm is the chic Café Opera and decide to go there in search of a steak, while Kian dithers. 'I think I'll just have a sandwich in my room,' he mutters. Then Bryan rushes over and announces happily, 'I've just paid the hotel chef fifty pounds to cook me a steak! But he's only going to do the two.'

Two steaks? Bryan then lands his mate right in it: 'Yeah, Kian asked him as well.' Kian looks shifty, while Anto and Nicky look appalled: 'You sneaky devil,' gasps Nicky. 'Whatever happened to "All for one and one for all"?'

Half an hour later, Nicky is settling into a big table in the Café Opera. The restaurant is quiet. 'Right,' says Nicky. 'We're going to tell Kian tomorrow that we had yummy steak and chips, and then that the Backstreet Boys and Max Martin came in and joined us! Just to make him sorry!' He laughs.

A few minutes later, the yummy steak and chips arrive — and, shortly after that, so do the Backstreet Boys! The band

A rare sighting of Nicky in the kitchen at Cheiron Studios, Sweden

sit down at the next table, and one of them stretches out his hand to Nicky, 'Hi, I'm Nicky,' he says. 'So am I,' answers a wide-eyed Nicky Byrne. And then someone else sits down. It's Max Martin . . .

Nicky just shakes his head. 'This sort of thing happens in Westlife all the time. One of us will wish for something, and it'll come true. We all wanted to be in a band, and we end up together. We all want a number one record, and we get five of them. We want to record with the best producers in the world, and here we are. We're an incredibly lucky band.'

The following evening, the whole band return to Café Opera with Louis, who has just flown in to hear the new songs. Shane orders steak – which reminds Anto . . . 'Emm, Shane,' he calls down the table. 'I've something bad to tell you. Remember you were giving out about the meat in the pasta? Well, I'm afraid it was horse meat . . .' Horse-loving Shane promptly turns green. Anto lets him suffer for a while, before admitting it was a joke.

The band stay out late that night – it's a rare chance for them to relax and chat with Louis. 'We've a great relationship with Louis,' explains Shane. 'I can talk to him about absolutely anything. It's not just a business arrangement: he's a friend too.'

As they stroll back to the hotel, dawn is lightening the sky over Stockholm, and Shane talks about the plans for the future. 'The year 2000 has been incredible so far, and we think that next year is going to be even better. We can't wait to start touring, and are already planning what the stage will look like, and what songs we'll do. We always have goals. We want ten number one singles, and we want to give our fans a brilliant second album. After all, without the fans, we'd be nothing.'

Profile: Nicky

FULL NAME:	**Nicholas (his mum calls him Nicholas at home!) Bernard James Adam Byrne**
DATE OF BIRTH:	**9 October 1978**
STAR SIGN:	**Libra**
MUM AND DAD:	**Yvonne and Nikki**
BROTHERS/SISTERS:	**Gillian and Adam**
HEIGHT:	**5ft 10in**
COLOUR OF EYES:	**Blue**
ANY SCARS OR TATTOOS?	**Two scars: one on my right elbow, and one on my left groin. One Celtic design tattoo across my lower back**

What do the rest of Westlife think of Nicky?

Shane: Nicky's a great guy. We're always planning stuff together – we'd love to open a restaurant or a club together. I can talk to Nicky about anything – he really listens and gives me proper advice. He's like an older brother and I look up to him an awful lot. He loves to shop as much as I do, and we've the same taste in clothes.

Bryan: Nicky's the friendly lad of the band. He'll talk to anyone. He's very smart and mature, and it takes a lot for Nicky to lose his head, even if everyone else is going mad around him.

Mark: Nicky has become a lot more laid back in recent

months. He used to worry about everything, but he's much more chilled now. And he's very stylish. He loves clothes, and, even if the rest of us look like we've been dragged backwards through a hedge, Nicky keeps it together.

Kian: He's a total professional, and always wants things to be right with the band. If he thinks he's right, he can be very stubborn. But he's a totally giving person, and really warm-hearted. This blue-eyed blond often looks as if butter wouldn't melt in his mouth. And it wouldn't melt – it would sizzle! For Nicky can talk the hind legs off a herd of donkeys! He's also a great hugger, and he loves getting the back of his neck massaged – it makes him purr with delight . . . And they say that the quickest way to a man's heart is through his stomach. This is certainly the case with our Nick, who loves his food – though his favourite meal is his mum's fry-up of bacon, sossies, the works! And lots and lots of tea . . .

Nicky in his own words

My favourite way to relax: There's a couch in the front room of my house, and I lie down on that and go to sleep. I love that couch! Mam's talked about getting rid of it, but I won't let her – I'd haul it out of a rubbish skip if I had to. And I love playing a few games of snooker with my mates, or hanging out with Georgina, watching videos and eating Chinese takeaway. I like to go out, but it can be hard in Ireland and Britain, 'cos you can feel people staring. Some are thrilled to see you, and some are cursing you. It can be very weird.

The worst moment of my life: The lowest point for me was in February 1998, when my cousin Kenneth was killed in a car crash. He was in a coma for a week before he died. He was only twenty-one. When he died, I went to the mass, but I had to miss burial, as the band — Westside as they were then — had our official launch in the Café de Paris in London. On stage that night, my heart wasn't in it. Sometimes I find his death very hard to accept. I dedicated the first album to him.

My first kiss: I think I was about nine years old, when I kissed the daughter of one of Mam's best friends in our back shed. But my first proper kiss was when I was about twelve, in the bushes with a girl from up the road. I felt a bit sick after it — but I got used to it very quickly!

Marriage: At one time, all the newspapers decided that Georgina and I were getting married. They even photographed Georgina's finger, which had a ring on it! But it was rubbish. I plan to get married eventually. I'd love to have kids and a family and a house, but not in the near future! But I've been brought up to believe that you grow up, settle down, have kids and live happily ever after.

Q&A
Who is your best friend in the band?
Nobody really, we all get on well, and I can go to any of the lads at any time about anything.
Are you a morning person or a night owl?
Definitely a night owl.
Do you read your horoscope?
No — I used to, but not any more.

Do you believe in aliens? If so, what do you imagine they look like?

Yes – I reckon they could look like Bryan!

What was the first record you ever bought?

Kylie Minogue's 'I Should Be So Lucky'.

How useful are you in the kitchen? What can you rustle up if you have to?

I can do a good Irish fry-up, but that's about it – I'm very good at opening the brown bag from the local chipper and putting the chips on a plate!

What part of your body would you change, if you could (keep it clean, lads)?

Nothing really – I wouldn't mind sorting out my bottom teeth, though!

Would you consider cosmetic surgery?

No, never.

Are you ticklish? If so, where (careful now)?

My neck is incredibly sensitive. Just someone touching it cracks me up!

What is the most expensive thing you've ever bought?

Probably my first car.

What is the most useless thing you've ever bought?

It's hard to decide! I've probably far too many pairs of shades and too many baseball caps.

What is the worst present you've ever received?

One Christmas I got a selection box from a girl who lived up the road from my house, and I had bought her a silver ring!

Have you ever been in hospital?

Yes, three times: once for a bad chest infection when I was young, and for two operations on a broken elbow and a hernia.

What is your favourite breakfast?

My mam's fry-up is out of this world!

Hangover cures – what is the most effective?

Anadin Extra – without them, my life would be over!

If you went on a blind date, who would you most like to find sitting on the bar stool?

Liz Hurley.

Have you ever written poetry?

No – the stuff I wrote in school was like 'The man in the van lived in a flat with his cat'!

What is your favourite TV programme?

Friends is so cool.

What is your favourite item of clothing?

My yellow leather trousers.

What is your most embarrassing item of clothing?

My yellow leather trousers!

What scares the living daylights out of you?

I worry about everything.

What is the last thing you lost?

I recently bought a book in Heathrow Airport, but left it in the shop, and only remembered it as the plane took off – and they wouldn't turn around and let me go back for it!

What is your favourite smoochy record?

Celine Dion's 'Because You Love Me'.

You've recorded with Mariah – who's next for a duet (or sextet, whatever)?

The Backstreet Boys.

Who is your favourite musician/actor/actress?

Sting or Phil Collins, Brad Pitt or Tom Cruise, and Meg Ryan.

What are the best/worst films you have ever seen?
Top Gun was the best. *Scream* was the worst.

What is the best book you have ever read?
Captain Fantastic by Mick McCarthy – it's the only one I ever finished!

Are you superstitious?
Yes – I'm superstitious about loads of things.

Did you enjoy school? What was your favourite subject?
School was a great laugh. I liked English and – eh – music!

What false name have you used in the past when checking into a hotel?
Mr White.

Do you have a lucky charm? If so, what is it?
I've loads of lucky and holy items that travel with me.

Are you romantic?
Yes – well, I like to think so!

Have you ever had your heart broken? If so, when, and by whom?
No, thank God – and if you're reading this, Georgina, no ideas, OK?

How old were you when you had your first kiss? Did you enjoy it?
I was about nine or ten. It was sloppy, but I thought I was cool!

Where is your favourite place in the world?
Dublin, Ireland.

Do you sing in the shower?
It depends on my mood.

Do you lose your temper easily?
Sometimes. I try to walk away, but on the football pitch I lose it all the time (I'm a very bad loser!).

Another Weekend with Westlife – Recording in Sweden

Do you cry easily?
No, unless someone close to me dies.
What is the worst job you ever had?
I've never had a bad job – I've only been a footballer, worked in a clothes shop and been a member of Westlife.
What is you favourite sport to watch and/or play?
Soccer.
If you weren't in a band, what do you think you'd be up to?
I'd just have finished my training to be a policeman, so probably some of the kids who like me now would avoid me!
What do you imagine your life will be like in ten years' time?
You never can tell!

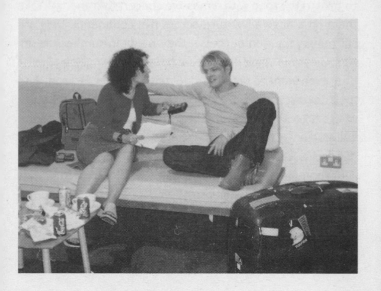

Epilogue

The year 2000 has been a magical year for the band, what Nicky describes as 'a roller-coaster ride of flights missed, and flights taken; of passports lost and of number-one hits around the world. It's been a year of great laughs and hard work. It's been pure magic.'

But the magic is only beginning. In 2001, Westlife are due to take to the road with a massive concert tour that will take them on a huge adventure across five continents. They are still hungry for more success – they want ten number one singles; they want their new album to sell by the millions. Hell – they even want to record a duet with Michael Jackson. And their dearest wish of all is to someday walk out on to the stage of the biggest venue in the heart of Dublin, the Gaelic football stadium, Croke Park, and play to a sell-out crowd – 'without getting bricked off the stage,' says Nicky.

Who is to say that their dreams won't come true? But even Nicky, Kian, Mark, Shane and Bryan can sometimes find it hard to grasp the Westlife whirlwind.

One evening last year, when the band were in Los Angeles, they, along with Ronan, were invited back to a house for a few drinks. They ended up wandering about a beautiful luxury mansion, perched high in the perfumed slopes of Beverly Hills. It was only after inspecting the photographs on the wall that they realised they were in George Michael's home. Mark and Anto strolled out on to the balcony, and leaned over, admiring the view. The vast spectacle of sparkling neon lights that is Los Angeles was spread far below them like a glowing carpet.

Mark gazed out in wonder, then turned to Anto: 'What's going on here? I'm from a small village in County Sligo, and two years ago I was listening to George Michael's records on the radio. Now I'm on his veranda. How did life suddenly get this crazy?'